The Scarlet Pimpernel
Study Guide

by Michael S. Gilleland & Eileen Cunningham

Limited permission to reproduce this study guide.

Purchase of this book entitles an individual teacher
to reproduce pages for use in the classroom or home.
Multiple teachers may not reproduce pages
from the same study guide.

This Progeny Press study guide may not be posted on the Internet in any form.

Exceptions:
- *Teachers may distribute this study guide file to students via email.*
- *Teachers may also, for the limited duration of a class, house files on a secure server with account-protected access and grant password-protected access to students. Students MUST have a password-protected account in order to access the files.*
- *This Progeny Press study guide may NOT be posted to or distributed via any file-share server that may be accessed publicly and/or accessible beyond the intended student class under any circumstances.*

For easier classroom or co-op use or distance learning with Progeny Press study guides, check out our interactive eGuide downloads, available at www.progenypress.com.

Table of Contents

Study Guide Authors

Michael S. Gilleland is president of MG Publishers Group LLC and publisher of Progeny Press. He has authored a number of study guides published by Progeny Press and edits all middle and upper level study guides. Mr. Gilleland graduated from the University of Wisconsin—Eau Claire with a Bachelor's Degree in English and Journalism. He spent his early career as a senior legal editor for a law book publisher and later created his own company specializing in book design and composition. Mr. Gilleland has served several turns as church elder and adult Sunday School teacher. He and his wife Rebecca homeschooled all of their seven children.

Eileen Cunningham teaches classical composition and humanities courses at the Classical School of Wichita in Wichita, Kansas. A fourth-generation Kansan, Mrs. Cunningham received her Bachelors degree in Secondary Education (emphasis in English) in 1968 and her Masters degree in European history in 1977, both from Kansas State University. In addition to experience in both public and private Christian high schools, Mrs. Cunningham also taught English as a Second Language at Wichita State University for 21 years. Occasionally, she also teaches composition courses for the University of Phoenix—Wichita. She is married to Patric Cunningham and has one adult son.

Note to Instructor

How to Use Progeny Press Study Guides. Progeny Press study guides are designed to help students better understand and enjoy literature by getting them to notice and understand how authors craft their stories and to show them how to think through the themes and ideas introduced in the stories. To properly work through a Progeny Press study guide, students should have easy access to a good dictionary, a thesaurus, a Bible (we use NIV translation, but that is up to your preference; just be aware of some differences in language), and sometimes a topical Bible or concordance. Supervised access to the Internet also can be helpful at times, as can a good set of encyclopedias.

Most middle grades and high school study guides take from eight to ten weeks to complete, generally working on one section per week. Over the years, we have found that it works best if the students completely read the novel the first week, while also working on a prereading activity chosen by the parent or teacher. Starting the second week, most parents and teachers have found it works best to work on one study guide page per day until the chapter sections are completed. Students should be allowed to complete questions by referring to the book; many questions require some cross-reference between elements of the stories.

Most study guides contain an Overview section that can be used as a final test, or it can be completed in the same way the chapter sections were completed. If you wish to perform a final test but your particular study guide does not have an Overview section, we suggest picking a couple of questions from each section of the study guide and using them as your final test.

Most study guides also have a final section of essays and postreading activities. These may be assigned at the parents' or teachers' discretion, but we suggest that students engage in several writing or other extra activities during the study of the novel to complement their reading and strengthen their writing skills.

As for high school credits, most Christian high schools to whom we have spoken have assigned a value of one-fourth credit to each study guide, and this also seems to be acceptable to colleges assessing homeschool transcripts.

Internet References

All websites listed in this study guide were checked for appropriateness at the time of publication. However, due to the changing nature of the Internet, we cannot guarantee that the URLs listed will remain appropriate or viable. Therefore, we urge parents and teachers to take care in and exercise careful oversight of their children's use of the Internet.

Synopsis

Originally produced as a stage play in 1903, *The Scarlet Pimpernel,* set during the Reign of Terror in the French Revolution, is the tale of a mysterious English nobleman who employs ingenious disguises to help French aristocrats escape execution at the guillotine. Assisting him is a band of other young English nobles; together they compose the League of the Scarlet Pimpernel. The revolutionary government of France is determined to track down these Englishmen, break up their campaign, and execute them. To determine the identity of the Scarlet Pimpernel, they send to England their agent Chauvelin to enlist the aid of Marguerite St. Just, a beautiful French actress who has married the foppish—but very wealthy—nobleman Sir Percy Blakeney, making her the center of aristocratic social life in England. Though Marguerite at first refuses to help, she is ultimately persuaded by Chauvelin's threat to kill her brother, Armand St. Just, who has joined forces with the Scarlet Pimpernel. The story takes many unexpected turns until Marguerite discovers the identity of the Scarlet Pimpernel and determines that she must find a way to save both the Englishman and her brother.

About the Novel's Author

Baroness Emma Orczy was born in Hungary in 1865, the daughter of Baron Felix Orczy. Due to political and economic problems, the Orczy family left Hungary, living temporarily in Brussels and in Paris before settling in London. Orczy was a quick language learner and spoke three languages fluently by the time the family arrived in London, where she learned her fourth language, English, the language she chose for her writing career.

As a young woman, Baroness Orczy loved to wear beautiful gowns and ostrich-feather hats, which she liked to employ as the splendid costume of her heroine, Marguerite St. Just, who is described in Chapter 4 as wearing a large hat with "undulating and waving plumes." Some believe that the character of Marguerite is Baroness Orczy's "alter ego," the personality she would have liked to be. The baroness and her husband were trapped in Monte Carlo by the Nazi invasion of World War II, during which time her husband, Montagu Barstow, died. After the war, she returned to England where she died in 1947. The Baroness wrote numerous books as well as an autobiography entitled *Links in the Chain of Life*. Other titles in the Pimpernel series include *The League of the Scarlet Pimpernel, The Elusive Pimpernel, I Will Repay, The Triumph of the Scarlet Pimpernel,* and *Eldorado: Further Adventures of the Scarlet Pimpernel.*

Background Information

The French Revolution and the Reign of Terror

The Scarlet Pimpernel, by Baroness Emma Orczy, is set during what might be called the second phase of the French Revolution, a period known in history as the Reign of Terror. It was primarily a "class war," in which members of the lower classes rose up against the nobility and the king, establishing a republic according to philosophical principles of the day regarding the equality of all men. The American Revolution preceded the French Revolution and, in many ways, served as a model for the republican constitution that eventually emerged in France. However, unlike the American Revolution of 1776, the French Revolution of 1789 led to a cruel period when 50,000 French men and women were put to death, most being innocent of any serious wrongdoing.

In 18th-century France, the population was classified into three legal entities called the Three Estates, which met (with unequal powers) to establish the laws of the kingdom in a parliamentary organization called the Estates-General (Etats-Generaux). The first estate was the French clergy, officials of the Roman Catholic Church such as bishops, archbishops, and cardinals. The second estate was composed of the French aristocracy, titled persons such as dukes and counts. Since the highest positions in the church were held by members of titled families, one might say that the aristocracy was doubly represented in the first and second estates. The third estate, however, was composed of the French commoners, by far the largest group, though the weakest politically.

The third estate had three quite different sub-groups: the peasantry, primarily landless men who worked land owned by others; skilled artisans and shopkeepers from the towns and cities; and the educated middle class, or bourgeoisie, which included doctors, lawyers, writers, public office holders—and actresses like Marguerite St. Just, heroine of *The Scarlet Pimpernel.*

What triggered the French Revolution was a series of crop failures in the 1780s that led to skyrocketing food prices and, ultimately, to starvation. This was compounded by a depression in manufacturing that led to unemployment among the urban poor. A series of maneuvers in the Estates-General did not lead to significant change, and in July and August of 1789, uprisings among both the rural and urban members of the third estate led to violent rebellion. The most historic confrontation was that of July 14, 1789, when members of the third estate "stormed the Bastille," a French prison and armory, setting free the prisoners (only seven actually were incarcerated at the time) and taking the weapons for use in their uprising. It is this event which is celebrated annually in France on July 14, the French Independence Day, still called Bastille Day.

This event was followed in October by a march on the palace of Versailles where King Louis XVI was staying with his wife, Marie Antoinette of Austria, and son Louis, who would have been Louis XVII if events had turned out differently. "Let us fetch the baker, the baker's wife, and the little baker's boy," the women cried, referring to the royal family, whom they held responsible for the extraordinary cost of bread. Armed with everything from broomsticks to muskets, the women of

Paris, soon joined by 20,000 sympathetic soldiers, demanded relief in bread prices in order to feed their starving children. The king and his family were taken into custody and marched back to Paris.

Despite numerous reforms which followed this event, unrest continued. Competing interests at home and reactions among the aristocracy in other European countries did not lead to the quick end of the revolution that some may have envisioned. Radical groups attacked the royal palace in August 1792, taking King Louis captive. In January 1793, the king was guillotined, and the execution of Marie-Antoinette followed in October. The execution of the king triggered a period in French history known as the Reign of Terror. For the next two years, thousands of people—many quite innocent—were rounded up and executed at the notorious guillotine and elsewhere. Actually, only about eight percent of those killed at the guillotine were aristocrats. The remainder were members of the middle class, the clergy, the peasantry, and the townsmen. The revolution came to an end after the execution of Maximilien Robespierre, the cruel mastermind of the Reign of Terror. Cooler heads in the revolutionary government feared that if they did not execute Robespierre, he eventually would execute them. As a result, on July 24, 1794, Robespierre died on the guillotine he had used so cruelly against others, effectively ending the period in European history known as the Reign of Terror.

Ideas for Prereading Activities

You may find additional extension activities, projects, and information on this and other Progeny Press titles at https://www.pinterest.com/progenypress/boards/.

1. With a map or atlas, locate England, France, and the English Channel. In England, locate London and Dover. In France, locate Calais and Paris.

2. Consult an encyclopedia or a reliable Internet source for information on King Louis XVI and Marie Antoinette, the French king and queen who were executed in the Reign of Terror. What was the history of the Bourbon dynasty? What was the theory of the divine right of kings? What happened to the son of Louis XVI after the executions of his mother and father?

3. Consult a history book to discover the causes, aims, and outcome of the French Revolution.

4. Find information in the library or on the Internet about Robespierre, the "mastermind" of the Reign of Terror. Who was he? How did he come to power? What happened to him in the end?

5. Consult a history book or sources on the Internet for information about the impact of the French Revolution on England. What was the position of King George? William Pitt, the Prime Minister? What were the views of Edmund Burke, author of *Reflections on the Revolution in France* (1790)? What and when were the Glorious Revolution and the Cromwellian Revolution in England?

6. Find a French-English dictionary and use it to look up French terms and pronunciations as you read the novel. If you do not understand the phonetic spellings in the dictionary, try to find another dictionary or an online dictionary or pronunciation guide to help you. Correct pronunciation can help you enjoy reading and discussing the novel. For instance, *citoyen* is pronounced "si-twa-yah'".

Chapter 1–5

Vocabulary:

A *synonym* of a word is another word that means the same or nearly the same thing as the first word. An *antonym* of a word is another word that means the opposite of the first word. For each of the vocabulary words below, write a synonym and an antonym to demonstrate your understanding of its meaning.

	Synonym	*Antonym*
1. seething		
2. carnage		
3. audacity		
4. impudent		
5. semblance		
6. inherent		
7. peremptory		
8. jovial		
9. effusive		
10. foppish		
11. reprobate		
12. enigmatic		
13. contemptible		
14. effusive		
15. inane		

Questions:

1. Who is the Scarlet Pimpernel and what does he do?

2. Why does Bibot allow the old woman in the cart to pass without inspection? Who is the old woman?

3. Who was hidden in the cart the old woman drove through West Barricade past Bibot?

4. Of what does the Comtesse accuse Marguerite St. Just?

5. Identify each character below by matching the name with the proper description.

___ Mr. Jellyband	a. English noble, escorted the De Tournays, attracted to Suzanne
___ Sally	b. English nobleman, full of life and laughter, popular
___ Lord Antony Dewhurst	c. Landlord of "The Fisherman's Rest"
___ Comtesse de Tournay	d. French noblewoman escaped from France, dislikes Marguerite
___ Suzanne de Tournay	e. Daughter of the Comtesse, school friend of Marguerite
___ Sir Andrew Ffoulkes	f. Daughter of the landlord of "The Fisherman's Rest"
___ Vicomte de Tournay	g. Former French actress, wife of Sir Percy Blakeney
___ Sir Percy Blakeney	h. Wealthy English nobleman, friend of the Prince of Wales
___ Marguerite St. Just	i. Brother of Marguerite, French republican in sympathies
___ Armand St. Just	j. Son of the Comtesse

Analysis:

6. Every story has a *voice* or *tone* that the author sets for the reader. The voice the author uses sometimes reflects the author's own attitude toward the characters and events, but often the author speaks with a voice different from her own and says things in the story that are contrary to her own viewpoint.

   In Chapter 1, Orczy adopts a voice in the writing that almost makes her a direct narrator, almost a character in the story. Do you think the voice and tone in the first few pages of Chapter 1 reflect the attitude and point of view of the author? How does the tone and viewpoint compare with the that of the following chapters? Why do you think Orczy wrote Chapter 1 in this way?

7. *Juxtaposition* is the act of placing two things side by side for comparison or contrast. An author uses juxtaposition to underscore the distinctive characteristics of two people, things, happenings, or places. What do you think the author may have been attempting to communicate to the reader by following the scene and events in Chapter 1 with the scene and characters in Chapter 2?

8. In literature, the term *stereotype* refers to a character with exaggerated characteristics intended to represent all members of his or her group. In *The Scarlet Pimpernel,* Mr. Jellyband is a stereotypical Englishman of the 18th century, sometimes referred to as John Bull as we might refer to John Q. Public or John Doe. From what you see in Chapter 2, what are some of the characteristics of John Bull?

9. *Irony* is a difference between appearance and reality, or between what is expected and what actually happens. *Dramatic irony* is when the reader sees a character's mistakes which the character is unable to see himself. Review Jellyband's interactions with the strangers playing dominoes in the corner of the coffee-room near the end of Chapter 2, and the strangers' actions at the beginning of Chapter 4. How is conversation between Jellyband and the strangers ironic? Would you classify Jellyband's conversation as irony or dramatic irony?

Dig Deeper:

10. Early in Chapter 3, Orczy writes that though the killing in France

> filled everyone in England with unspeakable horror, the daily execution . . . seemed to cry for vengeance to the whole of civilised Europe. . . . Mr. Pitt, with characteristic prudence, did not feel that this country was fit yet to embark on another arduous and costly war. It was for Austria to take the initiative . . . and surely 'twas not—so argued Mr. Fox—for the whole of England to take up arms, because one set of Frenchmen chose to murder another.

The positions and statements Orczy attributes to the English politicians are often used by people facing all kinds of large and small conflicts. We often hear that the problems in another family or between neighbors are none of our business, we need to let *them* resolve it, or that the conflicts in neighboring nations or regions are too costly for us to get involved. Are these arguments valid? How can we decide when and how to get involved in and try to solve the conflicts of others?

11. Briefly summarize how Marguerite acts when she sees the Comtesse and Suzanne in the coffee-room, the Comtesse's response to Marguerite, and Marguerite's response to the Comtesse. Based on Marguerite's actions, do you think Marguerite is guilty of the things of which the Comtesse has accused her? What are your impressions of Marguerite's character?

12. What assumptions does Jellyband make about his own powers of discernment concerning being fooled by French spies? What effect does this have on his assumptions about the strangers playing dominoes and his assertions to Lord Anthony?

13. Compare the attitudes of Bibot and Jellyband concerning their own abilities. What do they think of themselves and their powers of perception? Read Proverbs 11:2, 16:18, and 1 Corinthians 10:11–12. Which one of these verses is quoted in the novel? How do these verses apply to Bibot and Jellyband?

Chapters 6–9

Vocabulary:

Write the letter of the correct definition from the box below in the blank next to the word it defines, then use the word in an original sentence of your own. Not all the definitions will be used.

Definition Box

a. dangerously, fatally

b. justifying, vindicating, exonerating

c. self-controlled, composed, calm, placid

d. heated, spirited, forcible

e. whole-hearted, fervent, enthusiastic

f. noble, grand, elevated

g. unemotional, unmoved, detached

h. center, heart, nucleus

i. reuniting, settlement, peace

j. perfect, wonderful, idealized

k. boredom, lethargy, dissatisfaction

l. unconventionality, quirkiness

m. deprived of, without

n. revenge, punishment

o. agile, capable, skilled

p. odious, revolting, repellent

q. observe, contemplate, scrutinize

r. creativity, imagination, artistry

_____   1. pivot   Sentence:

_____   2. malignantly   Sentence:

_____   3. eccentricity   Sentence:

_____   4. imperturbable   Sentence:

_____   5. reconciliation   Sentence:

_____ 6. vehement   Sentence:

_____ 7. lofty   Sentence:

_____ 8. extenuating   Sentence:

_____ 9. bereft   Sentence:

_____ 10. ardent   Sentence:

_____ 11. retribution   Sentence:

_____ 12. passive   Sentence:

_____ 13. idyllic   Sentence:

_____ 14. ennui   Sentence:

_____ 15. noisome   Sentence:

_____ 16. dexterous   Sentence:

_____ 17. ingenuity   Sentence:

Questions:

1. Why were people so surprised that Marguerite married Sir Percy Blakeney? What did they suppose were Marguerite's motives?

2. What reason does Marguerite give for marrying Sir Percy? Does she love him?

3. Why has Sir Percy seemed to have lost his love for Marguerite?

4. How was Armand St. Just connected to the Marquis de St. Cyr and his family? What happened to the St. Cyr family and what part did Marguerite play in what happened?

5. Why is Marguerite anxious for Armand as he returns to France?

6. What does Chauvelin discover in the letters taken from Sir Andrew and Sir Anthony?

Analysis:

7. Considering all we know about Marguerite's role in the death of the Marquis de St. Cyr, do you think she is guilty of his murder or for his execution, as the Comtesse does and, apparently Sir Percy does? Why or why not?

8. A *paradox* is a statement that seems to contradict itself, but is true or still makes sense. In Chapter 6, Orczy writes, "Everyone knew that [Sir Percy] was hopelessly stupid," yet a few sentences later writes, "Thus society accepted him, petted him, made much of him, since his horses

were the finest in the country, his *fêtes* and wines the most sought after." Earlier in the chapter, Sir Percy is described as much admired and copied for his style. What is paradoxical about these statements?

9. In these chapters Marguerite St. Just, her brother Armand, and others are identified as republicans. Look up *republic* in an encyclopedia and summarize the explanation of a republic.

Based on this, what would republicans believe and why would it be contrary to the former French monarchy and aristocrats such as the Comtesse de Tournay?

10. Consider the actions of the crowds in Paris, both in Chapter 1 and in descriptions throughout these chapters. What seems to be the motivating factor? Compare and contrast these motivations with Marguerite's in her exposing the Marquis de St. Cyr's actions.

11. *Foreshadowing* is a hint or clue an author gives about something that may happen later in a story. At the end of Chapter 6, Orczy writes,

> Only Sir Andrew Ffoulkes . . . noted the curious look of intense longing, of deep and hopeless passion, with which the inane and flippant Sir Percy followed the retreating figure of his brilliant wife.

What might the author be foreshadowing?

12. When an author wants to create suspense and encourage the reader to read on quickly to discover what will happen next, she often will use a technique called a *cliffhanger.* A cliffhanger usually is used at the end of a chapter or other potential stopping point and uses foreshadowing, introduces something new, or breaks away in the middle of the action to excite the reader and make him continue reading because he wants to know what happens next.

    Look at the end of Chapters 6, 8, and 9. How does the author use a cliffhanger at the end of each chapter to encourage the reader to keep reading?

Dig Deeper:

13. Review Marguerite's role in the Marquis de St. Cyr's execution. Should we be held accountable for bad things that happen because of our actions, even if we did not foresee or intend those things to happen? Explain your answer using Marguerite's situation.

14. Read Leviticus 19:18, Matthew 22:37–39, Romans 12:17–19. What do these verses warn us against? What are we supposed to do instead? How would things have been different for Marguerite if she had followed these verses?

15. Review Marguerite's reflections on her marriage with Sir Percy in Chapters 7 and 8. What does she want above all else from Sir Percy? Because she does not get this from him, how does she treat him in these chapters?

16. Read Ephesians 5:21–33. According to these verses, how should a husband treat his wife? How is a wife to respond to her husband? How does this compare to what Marguerite wants from Sir Percy? How do her actions and attitude toward Sir Percy compare to these verses?

Optional Activities:

1. Many times bad things happen in which we are involved to a greater or lesser degree. We may attend a party in which there is drinking, and a friend or acquaintance may be injured or killed because of driving under the influence. We may suspect or know of the physical abuse of a friend or family member but we do not speak out, and the friend or family member continues to suffer abuse. We may tell a secret and then see a person become humiliated or have his or her reputation damaged when the secret becomes public or is misunderstood. As a group, discuss similar situations and how we can decide when we should act and when we should not. What standards should we use to judge our own actions? How can we decide what is "our fault" and what is just the bad circumstances of life?

2. Discuss how Marguerite views marriage, or at least her marriage to Sir Percy. What does she think should be put into it; what does she think are her responsibilities and Sir Percy's responsibilities? Do you think they are realistic and healthy? What do you expect from marriage? Make an outline of the most important thing about marriage, then list each person's responsibilities and expectations. Back up your statements with scripture where possible.

3. *Discussion:* The passage in Ephesians 5 has become very controversial because of the directions to wives. What is the command in verse 21? If we follow that verse first and foremost (understanding that submission does not mean allowing abuse), how would that work in a relationship? How can two people submit to one another?

Chapters 10–13

Vocabulary:

A word is *in context* if we read it in the sentence in which it was written. It is out of context when it is by itself. The following underlined words are shown in the context of the sentences in which they appear in the book. Read the sentences and try to define the underlined words from the context. Then look up the dictionary definition and compare.

1. "The house was packed, both in the smart orchestra boxes and the pit, as well as in the more <u>plebeian</u> balconies and galleries above."

   Your definition:

   Dictionary definition:

2. "Evidently the one face she wished to see was not there, for she settled herself down quietly behind her mother, listened <u>apathetically</u> to the music, and took no further interest in the audience itself."

   Your definition:

   Dictionary definition:

3. "Two days ago the *Day Dream* had returned from Calais, bringing her news that her idolised brother had safely landed, that he thought of her, and would be <u>prudent</u> for her sake."

   Your definition:

   Dictionary definition:

4. "Marguerite turned quickly, in alarm, which was not altogether <u>feigned</u>."

   Your definition:

   Dictionary definition:

5. "'Three minutes in the privacy of this box are quite sufficient for me,' he rejoined <u>placidly</u>."

   Your definition:

   Dictionary definition:

6. "'Faith!' she added, <u>ostentatiously</u> smothering an imaginary yawn, 'had you not spoken about my brother. . . .'"

   Your definition:

   Dictionary definition:

7. "Marguerite sat, straight upright, rigid and <u>inert</u>, trying to think, trying to face the situation, to realise what had best be done."

   Your definition:

   Dictionary definition:

8. "'Fie! two very ugly words, fair lady,' protested Chauvelin, <u>urbanely</u>."

   Your definition:

   Dictionary definition:

9. "And in her eyes the <u>astute</u> Frenchman, read, no doubt, something which caused him profound satisfaction, for, with a sarcastic smile, he took a delicate pinch of snuff, then, having dusted his dainty lace jabot, he rubbed his think, bony hands contentedly together."

Your definition:

Dictionary definition:

10. "He and the few young jackanapes under his command, well furnished with money, armed with boundless daring, and <u>acute</u> cunning, had succeeded in rescuing hundreds of aristocrats from France."

Your definition:

Dictionary definition:

11. "And tonight, having delivered himself of his *bon mot*, he had left Marguerite surrounded by a crowd of admirers of all ages, all anxious and willing to help her to forget that somewhere in the spacious reception rooms, there was a long, lazy being who had been fool enough to suppose the cleverest woman in Europe would settle down to the <u>prosaic</u> bonds of English matrimony."

Your definition:

Dictionary definition:

12. "'For shame, Sir Andrew,' she said, shaking her head with a playful sigh, 'making <u>havoc</u> in the heart of some impressionable duchess, whilst conquering the affections of my sweet little Suzanne.'"

Your definition:

Dictionary definition:

Questions:

1. What does Chauvelin ask Marguerite to do at Lord Grenville's ball, and how does he persuade her to do it?

2. What ruse does Marguerite use to see the note Sir Andrew is reading?

3. What does Marguerite learn from the note?

Analysis:

4. Early in Chapter 10, Orczy writes,

> In Lord Grenville's box, too, a curious, interesting personality attracted every-one's attention; a thin, small figure with shrewd, sarcastic face and deep-set eyes, attentive to the music, keenly critical of the audience, dressed in immaculate black, with dark hair free from any powder.

Who is this character? Since we have met this person several times before, why do you think the author introduces him again this way, rather than introducing him by name?

5. In Chapter 10, the Comtesse de Tournay says to Lord Grenville, "if this Chauvelin wishes to do us mischief, he will find a faithful ally in Lady Blakeney." Her friend, Lady Portarles, takes her to task:

> Lady Blakeney may or may not be in sympathy with those Ruffians in France; she may or may not have had anything to do with the arrest and condemnation of St. Cyr, . . . but she is the leader of fashion in this country; Sir Percy Blakeney has more money than any half-dozen other men put together, he is hand and glove with royalty, and your trying to snub Lady Blakeney will not harm her, but will make you look a fool.

Do you think Lady Portarles is wise in her advice, or is she being hypocritical? Are there times when her advice should be followed and times when it should not? Explain your reasoning.

6. *Similes* and *metaphors* are figures of speech that state or imply a comparison between two unlike things that have something in common. A simile uses words such as *like* or *as* to compare. One thing is said to be *like* another thing. A metaphor does not use these comparison words. One thing is said to *be* another thing. Before each of the following sentences, put an S if it contains a simile and an M if it contains a metaphor.

    _____ He paused a moment, like a cat which sees a mouse running heedlessly by, ready to spring, yet waiting with that feline sense of enjoyment of mischief.

    _____ Chauvelin was putting the knife to her throat.

    _____ Marguerite felt herself entangled in one of those webs, from which she could hope for no escape.

    _____ . . . virtue is like precious odours, most fragrant when crushed.

7. What feeling for her husband does Marguerite have at the beginning of Chapter 12? What does this reveal about how Marguerite views her marriage?

8. *Onomatopoeia* is a term for a word that sounds like the sound it describes; for example, *boom* for an explosion or *hiss* for an air leak. In Chapter 12, Orczy mentions "the frou-frou of rich dresses." Look up the word *frou-frou*. What does the word mean? Why might this word be onomatopoeia?

Dig Deeper:

9. A *moral dilemma* is defined as having to make a choice between two things that are either both right (something one should do) or both bad (something one should not do). The result being that no matter what one does, the consequence is either painful or morally unacceptable. This is

often referred to as being "between a rock and a hard place," because both options are hard and painful. In Chapter 10, Chauvelin confronts Marguerite with a moral dilemma: should she act to save her brother, or should she refuse to act and save the Scarlet Pimpernel and French aristocrats. She should save both her brother and protect the Scarlet Pimpernel; however she cannot do both.

What appears to be Marguerite's choice at the end of these chapters? Do you think she chooses wisely? What would you have done? Why?

10. Each of us has faced or will face moral dilemmas in our lives. For example, perhaps someone is being bullied in school or the neighborhood, but he or she has asked you not to tell. Do you keep their secret and allow the bullying to continue or do you betray their trust and do you tell someone in an effort to stop the bullying? Two friends are going on a mission trip and both need support, but you can afford to help only one. A family member or good friend is broke and needs a place to live for awhile, but you know that any money they get will go toward alcohol or drugs and they will bring that lifestyle into the home. Do you help them and let them stay with you, or do you protect your family (and possibly your friend) by refusing them shelter?

Have you ever faced a moral dilemma in your life? What was it and how did you decide what to do? How do you decide what to do when you are faced with a moral dilemma?

11. In Chapter 10, after Chauvelin confronts Marguerite with his ultimatum, Orczy says "she longed to seek comfort and advice from someone who would know how to help and console"; she wanted help in figuring out what the best course would be. Read Joshua 1:8, Proverbs 19:20, 2 Timothy 3:14–17, and James 1:5–6. How do these scriptures help someone seeking to discern the correct course of action? What criteria should we use when deciding how to choose in a moral dilemma, when all our choices may seem bad?

12. In Chapter 11, as the Prince is about to be introduced to the Comtesse de Tournay, he and Marguerite have the following exchange:

> ". . . she looks very virtuous and very melancholy."
>
> "Faith, your Royal Highness," she rejoined with a smile, "virtue is like precious odours, most fragrant when it is crushed."
>
> "Virtue, alas!" sighed the Prince, "is mostly unbecoming to your charming sex, Madame."

Review the paragraph or two leading up to this exchange, and consider previous descriptions of the Comtesse. Look up the definition of *virtue*, then look up *self-righteous*. Do you think the Prince and Marguerite were really discussing virtue or self-righteousness?

If they were discussing virtue, do you think they are right? How about if they were discussing self-righteousness? Have you ever encountered self-righteousness? How did it feel? Did it make you want to be better? Have you encountered true virtue? Did it make you want to be better?

Chapters 14–18

Vocabulary:

Underline the word on the right that is closest in meaning to the vocabulary word on the left.

1. cuisine	knife	food	questioning
2. incessant	ceaseless	foolish	under-valued
3. extricate	foul	decorate	extract
4. endeavor	dock	contract	attempt
5. audacity	inept	boldness	loud
6. elusive	ambiguous	thin	foggy
7. replica	reply	copy	request
8. benignly	agreeably	flexibly	malignantly
9. listless	disorganized	questionable	lethargic
10. subtle	textured	illuminated	muted
11. sarcastic	angry	contemptuous	beseeching
12. unerring	whitefish	unfailing	incorrect
13. tumultuous	turbulent	overheated	echoing
14. obstinate	fruit	stubborn	trapped
15. duped	deceived	copied	injured
16. caprice	lace kerchief	payment	whim
17. contradictory	opposing	complicated	same

Questions:

1. Who does Chauvelin expect to see in the supper-room at one o'clock? Who does he find there, and what is that person doing?

2. What does Sir Percy do when Marguerite tells him of her fears for Armand and Armand's danger?

3. What confuses Marguerite about Sir Percy's study?

4. What does Marguerite find in Sir Percy's study? What does it imply?

Analysis:

5. These chapters are full of similes and metaphors as Orczy describes events at the ball and Marguerite's predicament. Below are some of the passages containing similes and metaphors. In the blanks before the passages, put an S for simile or an M for metaphor. Some passages have more than one descriptive phrase.

   a. _____ It seemed to Marguerite that through all the noise, all the din of music, dancing, and laughter, she could hear his cat-like tread, gliding through the vast reception-rooms. . . .

   b. _____ . . . the chairs—turned towards one another in groups of twos and threes—seemed like the seats of ghosts, in close conversation with one another.

   c. _____ . . . there were chairs straight up in a row that still looked starchy, critical, acid, like antiquated dowagers. . . .

   d. _____ _____ . . . the hum of distant talk and laughter, and the rumble of an occasional coach outside, only seemed to reach this palace of the Sleeping Beauty as the murmur of some flitting spooks far away.

   e. _____ _____ . . . she knew that her woman's penetration would at once recognise in the stranger's face . . . that strong individuality which belongs to a . . . hero: to the mighty, high-soaring eagle, whose daring wings were becoming entangled in the ferret's trap.

   f. _____ _____ . . . the irony of that fate seemed so cruel which allowed the fearless lion to succumb to the gnawing of a rat!

   g. _____ . . . And having failed to trap the eagle once again, his revengeful mind would be content with the humble prey—Armand!

   h. _____ _____ _____ And stepping aside, he allowed the moths to flutter more closely round the candle, and the brilliant throng . . . eagerly attentive to Lady Blakeney's every movement, hid the keen, fox-like face from her view.

   i. _____ The river wound in and out in its pretty delicate curves, looking like a silver serpent beneath the glittering rays of the moon.

6. At the beginning of Chapter 15, Orczy writes of Marguerite,

> She wished she were in the supper-room, too, at this moment, watching him as [the Scarlet Pimpernel] entered; she knew that her woman's penetration would at once recognize in the stranger's face—whoever he might be—that strong individuality which belongs to a leader of men—to a hero: to the mighty, high-soaring eagle, whose daring wings were becoming entangled in the ferret's trap.

Briefly summarize what Marguerite is thinking in this paragraph. Knowing what we know, or believe, at the end of Chapter 18, why is this paragraph highly ironic?

7. *Hyperbole* (hi PER bo lee) is a term meaning extravagant exaggeration. Hyperbole is often used for emphasis, humor, or irony. Review the last paragraph of Chapter 17. How does Orczy use hyperbole in this passage to emphasize a change in Sir Percy?

8. *Romanticism* is a literary form that focused on the individual, emphasizing emotion, imagination over realism, sympathy for the common man, and the purity of nature, among other things; it did not deal with romance or love as we now tend to associate it. Romanticism as a genre or movement had its peak in the late 18th century and early 19th century, but its influences can still be seen in some passages and works. What about the last paragraph in Chapter 17 could be considered romantic in the literary sense?

9. An *allusion* is a brief reference to a literary or historical person or event with which the reader is assumed to be familiar. Authors can add meaning to a story by drawing upon the thoughts and feelings a reader associates with the allusion. In Chapter 18, Orczy refers to "Blue Beard's wife" and "Blue Beard's chamber." Look up Bluebeard (usually spelled as one word). Summarize the story of Bluebeard in a few sentences. Why do you think Orczy alludes to this story at this point in the novel?

10. Based on what Marguerite finds at the end of Chapter 18, who is the Scarlet Pimpernel? Thinking back on previous chapters, what clues did the author give that might have hinted that this person is the Scarlet Pimpernel?

Dig Deeper:

11. It can be easy to believe that we fully understand a situation or a person or that we can recognize good or evil when we see it, but like Marguerite we have totally misunderstood the situation. Has this ever happened to you? What happened? How can we avoid acting on such misunderstandings? (You may wish to review some of the scriptures from the Dig Deeper portion of the previous section of this study guide.)

12. Several times in these chapters, Orczy implies that Marguerite believes Fate has determined her situation:

    "Fate had willed it so." (Ch. 14)

    ". . . well! there, let Fate decide." (Ch. 14)

    "Fate *had* decided, had made her speak, had made her do a vile and abominable thing, for the sake of the brother she loved." (Ch.14)

    "How thoroughly a human being can be buffeted and overmastered by Fate had been borne in upon her with appalling force." (Ch. 16)

    ". . . the Marquis de St. Cyr had perished through a thoughtless words [sic] of hers; but in that case she was morally innocent—she had meant no serious harm—fate merely had stepped in." (Ch. 16)

    Look up the definition of *fate*. Do you think "Fate" has determined what has happened to Marguerite? Review the last two statements above and their context in the story. If "fate . . . had stepped in," would Marguerite be responsible for her actions?

13. The concept and understanding of fate can be an important and complicated one. In Christianity, fate, or determinism, is similar to a concept called *predestination,* the belief that God predestines or predetermines what will happen in our lives. Some people believe that God has predestined everything and some believe that we have purely free will. Read the following verses and summarize your impressions based on them: Proverbs 139:13–16, 16:9, 19:21; Romans 8:28–30; Ephesians 1:4–6; James 4:13–16; Genesis 4:6–7; Deuteronomy 6:18–19, 24–25; Proverbs 1:29–33; Galatians 6:7; James 4:4–7.

14. In Chapter 18, Sir Percy and Marguerite have a long discussion on the lawn shortly before dawn. As they talk, what does Orczy, and Marguerite, say is the cause of their marital discord and the tension between them? Do they overcome it? Read Ephesians 5:21–33. How could they have responded differently in their marriage to overcome this problem in the beginning?

Chapters 19–21

Vocabulary:

Choose the word from the box below that best completes each sentence. One or more synonyms for the missing word is given in parentheses.

Word Box		
quandary	wizened	raiment
vestige	poignancy	compunction
consummately	seclusion	paltry
delude	dulcet	remorse
appalling	indefatigable	atone
boisterous	trivial	profound

1. With the ring tightly clutched in her hand, she had run out of the room, down the stairs, and out into the garden, where in complete _____ *(solitude, privacy, secrecy)*, alone with the flowers, and the river and the birds, she could look again at the ring, and study that device more closely.

2. It was ridiculous! she was dreaming! her nerves were overwrought, and she saw signs and mysteries in the most _____ *(unimportant, inconsequential)* coincidences.

3. Had he already laid his plans for catching the daring plotter, red-handed, in France, and sending him to the guillotine without _____ *(scruples, misgivings, doubts)* or delay?

4. The mask of the inane fop had been a good one, and the part _____ *(supremely, expertly, perfectly)* well played.

5. Child as she was, she felt the _____ *(sorrow, mournfulness, misery)* of her friend's grief, and with the infinite tact of her girlish tenderness, she did not try to pry into it, but was ready to efface herself.

6. Her love for him had been _____ *(small, meager, inadequate)* and weak, easily crushed by her own pride; and she, too, had worn a mask in assuming a contempt for him, whilst, as a matter of fact, she completely misunderstood him.

7. By her own blindness she had sinned; now she must repay, not by empty _____ *(regret, guilt, repentance)*, but by prompt and useful action.

8. A change of _____ *(clothing, outfit)*, and a farewell to little Suzanne, and she could be on her way.

9. She did not attempt to _____ *(mislead, deceive, trick)* herself with any vain and futile hopes; the safety of her brother Armand was to have been conditional on the imminent capture of the Scarlet Pimpernel.

10. Marguerite had laid aside every _____ *(touch, hint, suggestion)* of nervousness; she was perfectly calm, and having returned the young man's elaborate salute, she began very calmly. . . .

11. I hope there are dangers, too!—I have so much to _____ *(make amends, pay for)* for.

12. He would not allow so _____ *(horrific, dreadful, abhorrent)* a crime to be committed, as the death of a brave man, through the hand of a woman who loved him, and worshiped him, and who would gladly have died for his sake.

13. Her coachman, too, had been _____ *(tireless, determined, persistent)*; the promise of special and rich reward had no doubt helped to keep him up, and he had literally burned the ground beneath his mistress' coach wheels.

14. Her coachman, whom she questioned, had not seen anyone answering the description his mistress gave him of the _____ *(wrinkled, shrunken, shriveled)* figure of the little Frenchman.

15. He evidently meant to wait up for Sir Andrew Ffoulkes, but was soon overcome by sweet slumbers, for presently—in addition to the slow ticking of the clock—Marguerite could hear the monotonous and _____ *(soothing, agreeable, melodic)* tones of the worthy fellow's breathing.

16. The wind was becoming _____ *(uproarious, unrestrained, uncontrolled)*, rattling the lead windows and the massive doors of the old-fashioned house: it shook the trees outside and roared down the vast chimney.

17. If we cannot cross over to France tonight, Chauvelin is in the same _____ *(predicament, trouble, dilemma)*.

18. Sir Andrew, with that _____ *(penetrating, perceptive, thoughtful)* sympathy born in all those who are in love, made her almost happy by talking to her about her husband.

Questions:

1. Although at the end of Chapter 18 and beginning of Chapter 19 Marguerite suspects the identity of the Scarlet Pimpernel, what information solidifies her suspicions? What makes her believe he is in immediate danger?

2. To whom does Marguerite go for help in her plans to save the Scarlet Pimpernel? Why does she ask for help, and why does she choose this person?

3. What does Jellyband think is going on when Sir Andrew joins Marguerite at "The Fisherman's Rest"? How does Sir Andrew help to put his mind at ease?

4. What stops Marguerite and Sir Andrew from crossing over to France during the night? Why is this also a form of good fortune?

5. How does Sir Andrew entertain Marguerite while they wait in "The Fisherman's Rest"? Why do you think he does this and what effect does it have on Marguerite?

Analysis:

6. *Anthropomorphism* is a technique by which an author gives human or animal characteristics to inanimate objects or concepts. For example, "The trees danced in the wind, a slow, sweeping ballet of stationary freedom," speaks of trees as if they are human dancers, giving them purpose in their movements. In Chapter 19, Orczy writes, "Surely Fate could not deal a blow like that: Nature itself would rise in revolt," and in Chapter 21 she writes, "Nature herself was playing a horrible, cruel trick." What does Orczy anthropomorphize in these sentences? How does she give human or animal characteristics to objects or concepts?

7. Near the middle of Chapter 19, Marguerite says about Sir Percy's actions as the Scarlet Pimpernel:

> [Percy rescued French aristocrats] all for the sheer sport and devilry of course!—saving men, women and children from death, as other men destroy and kill animals for the excitement, the love of the thing. The idle, rich man wanted some aim in life—he, and the few bucks he enrolled under his banner, had amused themselves for months in risking their lives for the sake of an innocent few.

According to this quotation, to what does Marguerite attribute Sir Percy's and his friends' motivations for rescuing the aristocrats of France? (See a similar discussion between Lord Antony and the Comtesse in the middle of Chapter 4.) Do you think this is an accurate interpretation of the reasons for his actions? Why?

Dig Deeper:

8. Review the quotation above from Chapter 19 and the referenced passage near the middle of Chapter 4. If the Scarlet Pimpernel and his men rescue French aristocrats purely for excitement, how would that affect your opinion of them? Why?

9. Define the words *altruism, self-interest,* and *egoism.* Below are listed a number of common sayings and Bible verses. In the blank before each saying or verse, write an A if the saying describes altruism or E if the saying describes egoism or self-interest.

altruism:

self-interest:

egoism:

a. _____ It's every man for himself.

b. _____ Love your neighbor as yourself.

c. _____ If it feels good, do it.

d. _____ All is fair in love and war.

e. _____ If someone forces you to go one mile, go with him two miles.

f. _____ Eat, drink, and be merry, for tomorrow we die.

10. Compare Marguerite's actions in these chapters with previous chapters. Would you consider her actions in previous chapters as altruistic or self-serving? How would you describe her actions in these chapters? What has changed?

11. Read Philippians 2:1–11. According to these verses, what is to be our primary motivation and attitude in life? Are we to totally avoid self-interest? What are we to use as our model and guide as we judge our own actions and attitudes?

Optional Activities:

Discuss as a class, or explore in an opinion paper, the issue of the importance of a person's motivations in their actions. If a person is doing something good, does it matter *why* they are doing it? Who would you trust more, an altruistic person or a person acting out of self-interest? If someone does benefit, does that automatically mean they are not acting altruistically? How should we ourselves act? Support your statements with examples from experience, the Bible, or other sources.

Chapters 22–26

Vocabulary:

A *thesaurus* is a book that lists words in groups of synonyms and related concepts. For each of the words below, write a definition using a thesaurus and then use the word in a sentence of your own to demonstrate your understanding of the word.

1. abate:

    Sentence:

2. conjecture:

    Sentence :

3. perfunctory:

    Sentence :

4. sordid:

    Sentence:

5. pretense:

    Sentence :

6. surly:

    Sentence :

7. imminence:

    Sentence :

8. apathy:

    Sentence :

9. dubiously:

    Sentence :

10. brusque:

    Sentence :

11. implicitly:

    Sentence:

12. malice:

    Sentence:

13. meager:

    Sentence:

14. suavely:

    Sentence:

15. fortitude:

    Sentence:

Questions:

1. What was the atmosphere and the attitude of the people in France and Calais when Marguerite and Sir Andrew arrive?

2. How does Brogard treat Marguerite and Sir Andrew?

3. What does Brogard tell them about Sir Percy?

4. Who comes into the "Chat Gris" after Sir Andrew leaves to look for Sir Percy? How is he dressed?

5. How does Sir Percy get out of the "Chat Gris" without Chauvelin capturing him?

6. Who knows something of where Sir Percy is going and is brought before Chauvelin? How does Chauvelin react to this person? How does he reward him?

Analysis:

7. Several times in these chapters the author refers to a tricolor cockade: "The men all wore red caps . . . but all with the tricolor cockade pinned on the left-hand side" (Ch. 22). Research the tricolor cockade and explain what a cockade is, what is significant about the tricolor cockade, and, if possible, explain the significance of pinning the tricolor cockade to the left side. What were the men communicating by wearing the tricolor cockade?

8. There are two words in Chapter 22 that could cause confusion because we in the United States and in this time do not often use them in the way the author uses them. Look up the underlined words in the following sentences and write down the definition that accurately reflects what the author means.

    a. ". . . one corner of the table was propped up with a bundle of <u>faggots</u>, there where the fourth leg had been broken." _____
    _____

    b. ". . . were it not for the earnestness of her purpose, [Marguerite] would <u>incontinently</u> have fled from this abode of dirt and evil smells." _____
    _____

9. Near the end of Chapter 24, Orczy uses a metaphor to describe Chauvelin's hopes for capturing Sir Percy, "The brave eagle, captured, and with noble wings clipped, was doomed to endure the gnawing of the rat." How does the author continue this metaphor into the next chapter? This metaphor again appears just before the incident of the snuff-box. What is different about each occurrence of this metaphor? Why do you think this is?

10. At the end of Chapter 24 and the beginning of Chapter 25, Percy enters the "Chat Gris" singing. What is he singing? Note the things Percy says to Chauvelin and the way he acts toward him in Chapter 25. Why do you think Sir Percy treats Chauvelin this way? How might his singing that particular song be connected to the way he treats Chauvelin?

Dig Deeper:

11. Throughout the novel, the Scarlet Pimpernel has been admired as the ultimate leader whose men would willingly die for him. In the middle of Chapter 23, Marguerite and Sir Andrew several times mention a character trait that helps explain the Scarlet Pimpernel's followers' great devotion. Give one quotation from this chapter illustrating their statements concerning this trait of Sir Percy and explain what the trait is.

12. Read Psalm 15 and Matthew 5:33–37. Paying particular attention to Psalm 15:2 and 4 and Matthew 5:37, what do these passages have in common with each other? What do they have to do with, and how do they impact, leadership qualities such as Percy's?

13. Review the actions and statements of Brogard in Chapter 22. What does Brogard seem to believe about freedom, and how does he express it in his words and actions? Use examples from the novel to explain your answer.

    Why do you think he behaves this way?

14. Read 1 Peter 2:9–25; Matthew 5:40–42; 1 Corinthians 6:5–7, 12; 10:23–24. Summarize and paraphrase what these verses are saying about freedom and how it should be exercised. How does this compare with Brogard's attitude toward and expression of his freedom?

Optional Activities:

1. Gather quotations about freedom and its exercise, then hold a class discussion, do a research paper, or create a bulletin board, mural, or poster discussing those sayings and what they mean. A bulletin board, mural, or poster can contain images that express or relate to the freedom quotations.

2. Write a paper or give an oral presentation about what freedom means in your own life. Discuss what it means in your day-to-day activities. You may also discuss what it will mean to you as you prepare to or after you graduate from high school and transition into adulthood.

Chapters 27–31

Vocabulary:

Read the sentence from the book, then answer the question about the underlined word by choosing the correct response.

1. "The air was keen and full of <u>brine</u>; after that enforced period of inactivity, inside the evil-smelling, squalid inn, Marguerite would have enjoyed the sweet scent of this autumnal night. . . ."

   If the air is full of brine, it is full of _____.

   a. fog

   b. breezes

   c. salt spray

   d. drizzle

2. ". . . she would have revelled in the calm and stillness of this lonely spot, a calm, broken only at intervals by the <u>strident</u> and mournful cry of some distant gull. . . ."

   If something is strident, it is _____.

   a. piercing

   b. gentle

   c. musical

   d. murmuring

3. "And ahead the rumble of the wheels, bearing an <u>implacable</u> enemy to his triumph."

   To be implacable is to be _____.

   a. gloating

   b. murderous

   c. unforgiving

   d. fearsome

4. "He rubbed his hands together, with content, as he thought of the web which he had woven, and through which that <u>ubiquitous</u> and daring Englishman could not hope to escape."

   The Englishman is ubiquitous because he is _____.
   a. mysterious
   b. ever-present
   c. foolish
   d. law-breaking

5. "She heard the soldier giving a few brief directions to the Jew, then she retired quickly to the edge of the road, and <u>cowered</u> behind some low shrubs, whilst Desgas and his men came up."

   To cower behind something is to _____.
   a. lay flat and unmoving
   b. study and observe
   c. restrain yourself
   d. crouch and shrink, shaking

6. "She felt neither soreness nor weariness; <u>indomitable</u> will to reach her husband in spite of adverse Fate, and of a cunning enemy, killed all sense of bodily pain within her, and rendered her instincts doubly acute."

   If one has indomitable will, one has a (an) _____ will.
   a. unshakable, determined
   b. tired, weary
   c. over-excited
   d. fickle, undecided

7. "He had <u>gauged</u> her very thoughts to a nicety."

   If someone has gauged something, they have _____ it.
   a. explained
   b. measured, evaluated
   c. directed, controlled
   d. wished for

8. "Something was thrown over her face; she could not breathe, and <u>perforce</u> she was silent."

   If something happens perforce to you, it happens _____.
   a. accidentally
   b. quickly
   c. unavoidably
   d. gently

9. "... with a rapid glance Chauvelin noted its contents: the cauldron placed close under an <u>aperture</u> in the wall, and containing the last few dying embers of burned charcoal. . . ."

   An aperture is a _____.
   a. slot, opening
   b. pipe, tube
   c. shelf
   d. stove

10. "The cleverest woman in Europe, the elegant and fashionable Lady Blakeney, who had dazzled London society with her beauty, her wit and her extravagances, presented a very <u>pathetic</u> picture of tired-out, suffering womanhood, which would have appealed to any, but the hard, vengeful heart of her baffled enemy."

    When something or someone looks pathetic, they look _____.
    a. clear
    b. laughable
    c. disgusting
    d. pitiful

11. ""Your Honour . . ." he ventured <u>imploringly</u>."

    If you implore, you are _____.
    a. pleading
    b. tired-out
    c. questioning
    d. angry

12. "With mock gallantry, he stooped and raised her icy cold hand to his lips, which sent a thrill of indescribable <u>loathing</u> through Marguerite's weary frame."

    If you are filled with loathing, you are filled with _____.
    a. sickness
    b. hatred
    c. numbness
    d. faintness

13. "'But those brutes struck you!' she gasped in horror, at the bare recollection of the fearful <u>indignity</u>."

    If something is an indignity, it is _____.
    a. pain
    b. disrespect
    c. a dangerous situation
    d. injury

14. "She remembered him now tardily and with a pang of <u>remorse</u>."

    If you feel remorse, you feel _____.
    a. fear, terror
    b. sadness, sorrow
    c. regret, repentance
    d. amusement, joy

Questions:

1. What does Marguerite do when Chauvelin leaves to find his way to Père Blanchard's hut?

2. Who acts as guide for Chauvelin, taking him to Père Blanchard's hut? How does Chauvelin repay the man?

3. What happens to the men waiting in the hut for Sir Percy? How does this happen?

4. What does Marguerite do when she hears someone singing "God Save the King"? Does this help or harm the Scarlet Pimpernel?

5. How does the Scarlet Pimpernel effect his final escape? What happens to Chauvelin?

Analysis:

6. Early in Chapter 27, the Jewish man tells Chauvelin, referring to the people they are supposed to be following, "I can see the imprint of the cart wheels, driven by that traitor, that son of the Amalekite." What allusion is he making? Who are the Amalekites, and why would the man call his competitor an Amalekite?

7. Read the following sentences and phrases and signify what kind of literary technique it is. In the blanks before the passages, write an S for a simile, M for a metaphor, and A for anthropo-morphism.

   a. _____ The road lay some distance from the sea, bordered on either side by shrubs and stunted trees . . . with their branches looking in the semi-darkness, like stiff, ghostly hair, blown by a perpetual wind.

   b. _____ Fortunately, the moon showed no desire to peep between the clouds. . . .

   c. _____ Everything around here was so still: only from far, very far away, there came like a long soft moan, the sound of the distant sea.

   d. _____ _____ . . . far away on her right was the edge of the cliff, below it the rough beach, against which the incoming tide was dashing itself with its constant, distant murmur.

   e. _____ Had then the tall stranger been sighted, and was this the mounted messenger, come to bring the great news, that the hunted hare had run its head into the noose at last?

   f. _____ Like a ghost she flitted noiselessly behind that hedge. . . .

   g. _____ _____ . . . warn them at any rate to be prepared and to sell their lives dearly, rather than be caught like so many rats in a hole.

   h. _____ He had played upon her feelings as a skilful musician plays upon an instrument.

8. Why did Sir Percy choose the disguise he did? Was it effective?

9. We have already seen that stereotype refers to a character with exaggerated characteristics intended to represent all members of his or her group. Look up *bigotry* and *prejudice*. How are these similar to, but distinctly different from, stereotype? How does bigotry and prejudice explain Chauvelin's attitude toward Rosenbaum?

Dig Deeper:

10. Early in the novel we examined a stereotype in the John Bull tradition. In these final chapters we see another stereotype in the Jew, Benjamin Rosenbaum. Beginning with the introduction of Rosenbaum in Chapter 26, list at least five stereotypical characteristics that the author, through Percy, gives the man.

11. How was Percy able to use Chauvelin's repugnance for Jews and Chauvelin's prejudice against them to accomplish his goal? What weakness did Percy exploit in Chauvelin?

12. Do you see stereotypes exhibited around you, in your home, school, work, friends? Is there a group or groups of people who are being viewed as all having the same characteristics, not as individuals? Do the stereotypes include bigotry and prejudice? Describe the situation and how that has affected the people involved.

13. Read Luke 10:25–37. Of what significance is it that the man who helped the wounded traveller was a Samaritan? (You may have to research the relationship between Jews and Samaritans at the time of Jesus.) What was Jesus trying to explain to his questioner? What does this mean to us?

Overview

1. For much of *The Scarlet Pimpernel,* the Blakeneys' marriage was unhappy, even somewhat contentious. Choose the character of either Marguerite or Percy and explain how the relationship and marriage progressed for that character. Examine how he or she falls in love, how and why he or she changes after the marriage, how he or she treats the spouse, and how the issues are finally resolved. Also briefly discuss whether you think that character was justified in his or her response in the marriage.

2. Review the way Baroness Orczy describes the attributes of men and women in this novel. Do you think she treats them equally or accurately? What do you think her attitude is toward the sexes? Use examples from the novel to explain your answer.

3. The main characters of a story are the *protagonists*. The forces working against the main characters are called the *antagonists*. The protagonists and antagonists take opposite sides in the conflict. Who are the protagonists and antagonists in *The Scarlet Pimpernel*? Who would you say is the main protagonist? Explain why.

4. A *false climax* is a way of increasing dramatic tension. In a false climax, the complication or danger reasserts itself after the author has led readers to believe that it has been resolved. An *epiphany* is a moment of sudden awareness, an insight that serves as a turning point for perception, or what we understand. In Chapters 18 and 19, Marguerite comes to the realization that Sir Percy is the Scarlet Pimpernel. In reviewing these chapters, do you think her coming to this understanding constitutes a false climax or an epiphany? Explain your reasoning.

5. In Chapter 27, Orczy says of Chauvelin,

> Never for a moment did the slightest remorse enter his heart. . . . As a matter of fact, Chauvelin had ceased even to think of [Marguerite]; she had been a useful tool, that was all.

List two examples from the novel in which Chauvelin demonstrates this attitude or behavior. What does this tell you about Chauvelin's character and attitude toward people in general? The Bible says "Do to others as you would have them do to you" (Luke 6:31). Clearly this is a command, but it can also lead to the corollary generalization, "People will treat you the way you treat them." How does Chauvelin's attitude and actions toward people affect their attitudes toward him? Use examples from the novel to demonstrate your answer.

6. A *foil* is an object or character who, by contrast, calls attention to or enhances the traits and qualities of another object or character. The opposite of a foil in literature is *parallelism,* purposefully using similar plots, characters, or other story elements to draw attention to and reinforce specific attributes, ideas, or patterns. Orczy sets a scene in an English inn in the early part of the novel, and then has a scene in a French inn near the end of the novel. Do you think Orczy is using these two inns and scenes as foils or as parallels? Why?

Compare and contrast the two scenes. What might Orczy be saying or implying about the situations in England and France by her descriptions of the two inns? Use examples from the book to illustrate your answer.

7. Clearly the theme of freedom threads its way throughout *The Scarlet Pimpernel,* but the author makes a point of bringing out one perspective on freedom in the passages concerning the "Chat Gris." Explain Brogard's apparent understanding of freedom, and then whether Brogard really is free, particularly in light of his actions and attitude after Chauvelin arrives. What might the author be implying about the freedoms in France during this time?

8. The *theme* of a novel is the main idea the author hopes to communicate to her readers through the story, though often more than one theme may be found in a work of literature. Select one of the following themes and explain how this theme is presented in the novel. What does the author seem to be saying about this subject?

love	leadership	moral dilemmas	heroism
moral responsibility	stereotypes	pride	prejudice
	revenge	nationalism	

9. Chauvelin and other French nationalists viewed the Scarlet Pimpernel and people who supported him as meddlers in national affairs that did not concern them. They believed that what the French did in France was no one else's business. Do you agree? Why? Does a country have the right to do whatever it wishes within its own borders? Do other countries, or citizens of other countries, have the right or responsibility to interfere in another nation's affairs? Explain your reasoning, using examples from the novel, history, or current affairs.

10. The term *willing suspension of disbelief* has come to be a literary term meaning that something generally impossible or implausible is made to seem plausible by the author's skill at telling the story. In a fairy tale, we are willing to believe that a prince will search the entire kingdom for a girl who fits a slipper, and the slipper fits only one person. A literary *contrivance* is a story element or plot development that seems unrealistic, but is necessary for the story to continue.

    What elements of the last few chapters of *The Scarlet Pimpernel* might be considered contrivances? Did they make it hard to suspend your disbelief or was Orczy successful in her story plotting?

Essays and Projects

You may find additional extension activities, projects, and information on this and other Progeny Press titles at `https://www.pinterest.com/progenypress/boards/`.

1. Baroness Orczy, the author of *The Scarlet Pimpernel,* lived during the time period when the infamous Dreyfus Affair occurred in France. In order to understand what Orczy would have known as French anti-Semitism, find information about this issue in the library or on the Internet. Write a two- to three-page paper explaining what happened in the Dreyfus Affair.

2. In a research paper, examine anti-Semitism in Europe in the late 19th and early 20th centuries. Explain its roots, how it manifested itself, and its ultimate expression in the European nations in World War II. As an alternative, you may research anti-Semitism in the world today, examining its roots, expression, and hot spots.

3. Review Overview question 9 and expand your answer into an opinion paper on national sovereignty. Include in your paper biblical references (such as Daniel 3, 6; Acts 4:5–21; Romans 13:1–3; Hebrews 13; and others), historical references, and references from current affairs. This may focus on national sovereignty or may be expanded to include citizens opposing their own governments.

4. In looking at scriptures relating to marital relationships and citizens' relationships with their governments, the word "submission" has arisen several times. Do a word study on "submission," examining how it is used and described in the Bible and how it is understood today.

5. Write a research paper comparing and contrasting the American and French revolutions. Some issues to consider: What political conditions preceded them and led to the revolutions? Who were the driving forces behind them? What were the philosophical and religious influences? What were their goals? How were the results similar and different?

6. The Scarlet Pimpernel was considered a great leader and commanded unquestioning loyalty among his followers. Write a paper examining what makes a great leader. You might look at historical leaders, look at biblical leaders and passages concerning leadership, and talk to leaders in your community.

7. Unfortunately, the indiscriminate killing of people of different ethnic background, faith, race, religion, or political affiliation did not begin with the French Revolution, nor did it end there. In a research paper or multimedia presentation, examine a period of genocide from history or current events. Discuss its origins, how it occurred, its justification, its results, and world reaction and response.

8. To oppose the killing of the old French aristocracy by the new French government, Sir Percy and his followers must have believed the actions of the French government were wrong.

However, Chauvelin, and many of Marguerite's former friends in France, believed the French government was completely justified in its actions. How can we decide what is truly right and wrong in such cases? Are there universal and absolute truths and right and wrong? Write a paper examining whether truth and right and wrong are absolute. Consider whether there are times in which some truths may command a higher priority than other truths. How do we know what is true and right? Do we have a right to impose truth on others or to hold others to our standards? You may wish to speak with your pastor, priest, or other religious leader to discuss your faith's perspective on truth and right and wrong. Also research other faiths' perspectives on these subjects, using the Internet, reference books, or personal interview for your research. This may be written as a formal research paper, but also may be produced as a series of video interviews or as a multimedia presentation.

9. As a group project, write and perform drama sketch in which Sir Percy and Marguerite go to a marriage counselor. This may be serious or humorous, but try to keep the issues and discussion as close to the story as possible, using dialogue and events from the novel whenever possible. This may be done as a video production or a live performance.

10. As an art project, draw, color, or paint a portrait of either Marguerite or Sir Percy. You might also do a landscape of the Père Blanchard's hut or Sir Percy's garden, or a picture of "The Fisherman's Rest" or "Chat Gris."

11. For a creative writing exercise, write a letter from Marguerite to Sir Percy while she is at "The Fisherman's Rest" impatiently waiting for the weather to turn so she can go to France.

Additional Resources

Other titles by Baroness Orczy	*Setting*
Most of the following titles are related to *The Scarlet Pimpernel.*	
The Laughing Cavalier	1623
The First Sir Percy	1624
The Scarlet Pimpernel	1792
Sir Percy Leads the Band	1793
The League of the Scarlet Pimpernel	1793
I Will Repay	1793
The Elusive Pimpernel	1793
Lord Tony's Wife	1793
The Way of the Scarlet Pimpernel	1793, concurrent with preceding two or three novels
Eldorado	1794
Mam'zelle Guillotine	1794
Sir Percy Hits Back	1794
Adventures of the Scarlet Pimpernel	1794
The Triumph of the Scarlet Pimpernel	1794
A Child of the Revolution	1794
Pimpernel and Rosemary	1917–1924

Film and Theater Adaptations of The Scarlet Pimpernel

The Scarlet Pimpernel	(1982) Starring Anthony Andrews, Jane Seymour, Ian McKellen
The Scarlet Pimpernel	(1999) Stuart Fox, Sarah Berger, Dalibor Sipek, and Suzanne Bertish
The Scarlet Pimpernel	Theatrical adaptation. Creative Classics Scripts

Other Titles of Interest:

Tale of Two Cities	by Charles Dickens
The Prisoner of Zenda	by Anthony Hope
The Three Musketeers	by Alexandre Dumas
The Man in the Iron Mask	by Alexandre Dumas
The Count of Monte Cristo	by Alexandre Dumas (also an abridged version by Puffin Classics)
The Prince and the Pauper	by Mark Twain
The Princess Bride	by William Goldman
King Solomon's Mines	by H. Rider Haggard

The Bronze Bow	by Elizabeth George Speare
The Adventures of Robin Hood	by Roger Lancelyn Green
Around the World in 80 Days	by Jules Verne
Treasure Island	by Robert Louis Stevenson
The Red Keep	by Allen French
To Say Nothing of the Dog	by Connie Willis
The Adventures of Sherlock Holmes	by Sir Arthur Conan Doyle

Answer Key

Note: Most of the questions in Progeny Press study guides deal with students' understanding and interpretation of issues in the novel; therefore, most answers will be individual to the student. Progeny Press answer keys are designed to be as inclusive as possible for the teacher and/or parent, giving enough background and information to judge whether the student has grasped the essence of the issue and the question. We try to point out some directions students' answers might take, which directions might be best, and some errors that may appear. Students are not expected to answer as completely as the answers provided in the Answer Key.

Chapter 1–5
Vocabulary:
Answers may vary but should be similar to the following suggestions: 1. swarming, churning; calm, quiet; 2. slaughter, massacre; opposites will vary, care, concern, peace, joy, accept reasonable choices; 3. insolence, defiance; submission, cooperation; 4. cheeky, impolite; polite, deferential; 5. disguise, facade; actual, real; 6. fundamental, built-in; add-on, act, affectation; 7. arrogant, commanding; polite, subservient; 8. cheerful, exuberant; miserable, grumpy; 9. unrestrained, lavish; restrained, self-controlled; 10. over-dressed, vain; plain, simple; 11. rogue, scoundrel; gentleman, an honest man; 12. mysterious, secret; open, expressive; 13. despicable, disgraceful; good, wonderful; 14. gushing, enthusiastic; quiet, silent; 15. silly, idiotic; sensible, well-mannered
Questions:
1. No one knows the true identity of the Scarlet Pimpernel, but he is an Englishman who rescues French aristocrats from the revolutionary government and guillotine. He also is the leader of a band of Englishman who follow his every order in rescuing French aristocrats.
2. Bibot allows the old woman to pass the barricade because she says her son may have the plague. She actually is the Scarlet Pimpernel, and the cart is filled with French aristocrats.
3. In the cart were hidden the Comtesse de Tournay and her two children, Suzanne and the Vicomte.
4. The Comtesse accuses Marguerite St. Just of betraying the Comtesse's cousin, Marquis de St. Cyr and his family to the French republican tribunal, which imprisoned and then executed them.
5. c; f; b; d; e; a; j; h; g; i
Analysis:
6. Answers may vary, but students should recognize that Orczy writes most of Chapter 1 with a perspective similar to that of the people of Paris and is not reflecting her own viewpoint. Her tone is sarcastic and ironic, saying such things as "those aristos were such fools! They were traitors to the people, of course, all of them, men, women, and children, who happened to be descendants of the great men who since the Crusades had made the glory of France." She is attempting to expose the foolishness of accusing even children of being traitors simply because of their ancestry. In later chapters Orczy writes in a much more direct and factual tone, though she often still writes with great irony. Answers may vary about why she writes the first chapter in this way, but it seems that she wants to set up and expose some of the illogic and contradictory thinking that was rampant at this stage of the French Revolution.
7. Answers may vary. Chapter 1 is filled with the turmoil, confusion, and bloodlust that was occurring in Paris at the time. Chapter 2 switches to a very different scene, a peaceful country inn on the English coast. In the inn, people are slowly going about regular lives: making and serving meals, flirting, needling one another in neighborly competition. Orczy is contrasting, and drawing attention to the extreme contrast between, the French situation and English situation at the time.
8. Answers will vary. John Bull seems to like to complain about many things and be a critic of things in England, yet believes anything English is better than anything foreign. He considers himself expert on many things and wily, yet has a very localized perspective on things. All in all, he seems generally happy, content, trustworthy, and trusting.
9. Answers may vary. The conversation between Jellyband and the strangers is ironic because they clearly are not who they appear to be. One of the strangers takes some pleasure in getting Jellyband to make some broad statements about French spies and Jellyband's ability to spot them and outwit or withstand them. He then insists on a toast with Jellyband after Jellyband asserts that he would not so much as drink a glass of ale with a Frenchman. Though our suspicions may be aroused in Chapter 2, they are confirmed in Chapter 4 when one of them hides under the bench. Accept either irony or dramatic irony. It clearly is irony, and definitely fits the dramatic irony definition, though generally dramatic irony is used in reference to a larger, more momentous irony.

Dig Deeper:

10. Answers will vary. This is a question that is difficult to answer in any definitive way because so many variables are involved. Sometimes getting involved in others' conflicts will only make things worse, yet sometimes outside intervention is necessary to resolve the problem. The issues are particularly troublesome when people's lives hang in the balance. The Bible repeatedly tells us as individuals to help the helpless, needy, and poor, but says very little about national responsibility.

11. Summaries will vary. When Marguerite enters the room, she is very happy and excited to see Suzanne and her mother, but the Comtesse refuses to acknowledge Marguerite and forbids Suzanne to speak with Marguerite. Marguerite looks slightly confused and hurt, but then acts rather haughty in return. Answers about Marguerite's guilt will vary. Her actions may make her appear innocent or may make her appear as if she does not think an accusation against the Comtesse's cousin, the Marquis, is a problem. So she could be innocent or cold-hearted. Her switch to haughtiness may make the reader lean toward cold-hearted. Answers about her character may be similar.

12. Answers will vary. Jellyband assumes that he can see through any French spies and their persuasive arguments. He even goes so far as to say that the warning in scripture about pride going before a fall does not apply to him because the writer of the proverb had never met Jellyband. He also likes the stranger because the man compliments Jellyband and flatters him, and because Jellyband assumes the stranger is safe, he drinks a toast with him, just after swearing he would never drink a toast with a French spy. Much more serious, however, is his assertion to Lord Anthony that the strangers are safe, even though he had no real evidence of it. This leads Lord Anthony to be much less cautious than he really needed to be.

13. Answers may vary. Bibot especially thinks quite highly of himself, pointing out the "foolishness" of the other gate-keeper, and implying that he would not have been fooled. Jellyband is very similar, stating that the French could not fool him as they have fooled his fellow innkeeper. Both consider themselves quite wise and sophisticated and able to see through disguises and trickery where others cannot. When Jellyband makes some of his claims, Hempseed says to him, "Let 'im 'oo stands take 'eed lest 'e fall," quoting from 1 Corinthians 10:12. These verses describe both Bibot and Jellyband quite well. Both think very highly of themselves and their powers of discernment, but both are just as likely to fail as others, and both do fail. Bibot fails to recognize and capture the Scarlet Pimpernel, and it is implied that he will go to the guillotine just as his fellow gatekeeper did. Jellyband is not found out as publically as Bibot, but the French spies clearly know he is being foolish, and his foolishness eventually leads some of his friends into danger.

Chapters 6–9
Vocabulary:
Sentences will vary. 1. h; 2. a; 3. l; 4. c; 5. i; 6. d; 7. f; 8. b; 9. m; 10. e; 11. n; 12. g; 13. j; 14. k; 15. p; 16. o; 17. r
Questions:

1. People were surprised that Marguerite, who was witty, smart, beautiful, popular, and French republican, would marry the English, aristocratic, silly, and apparently empty-headed Sir Percy. Many believed it was for his money and title, others believed it was just a whim or eccentricity.

2. Marguerite says she longed to be worshiped, and thought that Sir Percy, because he was stupid and not at her level of intellect, would worship her all the more completely. Answers will vary about whether she loves him. She seems to deeply desire to be loved by Sir Percy, and her feelings seem confused, particularly now that he seems to no longer love or admire her, but she does not seem to actually love him. The desire to have him love her has led her to ridicule him and punish him in public to get him to react.

3. Sir Percy seems to have lost his love for Marguerite when he learned that her denunciation led to the arrest and execution of St. Cyr and his entire family.

4. Armand loved Angèle de St. Cyr and wrote a love poem to her. However, Armand is a commoner and so the Marquis de St. Cyr had Armand severely beaten for daring to make advances to his daughter. For this Marguerite hated the Marquis, and when she heard that the Marquis was communicating with Austrian authorities encouraging them to come to the aid of French aristocrats, Marguerite mentioned it to her friends hoping to destroy his reputation. However, some of her friends had the Marquis arrested, confirmed the communications with Austria, and executed him and his family. Marguerite tried to stop the executions when she learned of them, but she could not.

5. Marguerite is anxious because although Armand works for the revolutionary government and shares, or shared, its goal of equality and justice, the situation is getting dangerous. People are denouncing others for small matters, and to even voice concern that the executions are getting out of hand and excessive is to risk being denounced as a traitor. Marguerite is afraid that Armand could be denounced despite his apparent loyalty to the new government.

6. Chauvelin discovers some of the plans for upcoming missions, but more importantly he learns that Marguerite's brother Armand is one of the followers of the Scarlet Pimpernel.

Analysis:

7. Answers will vary. Clearly Marguerite is guilty of betraying the Marquis de St. Cyr to the French republican authority; she told them about his ties to and communications with the Austrian government. She told them what she knew in hopes of getting him in trouble, in a spiteful spirit. However, she did not intend that the Marquis should be executed, and she definitely did not want the entire family to suffer or die. She tried to stop the executions but could not. So students may rightfully say that she is guilty because she betrayed them, but they also may be justified in saying she is not guilty because she did not intend their deaths and she tried to stop them.

8. It is paradoxical that people consider Sir Percy "hopelessly stupid" but admire his taste and copy his actions. It also is paradoxical that even though Sir Percy is considered stupid, he has the best horses and wines and has the best parties. It is a paradox that a man who is stupid could have such fine taste and acquire fine things.

9. Answers may vary; accept reasonable variations. A republic is a form of government based on representatives of the people of the nation. Generally those representatives are elected by the public, but they may also be elected or appointed by the public's elected representatives. Republicans, in its generic usage and as used in the novel, refers to people who believe in individuals' rights, civil rights, representative government, equality of all citizens, and the rule of law. These beliefs would be contrary to the monarchy and aristocratic rule because those were based on a class system in which wealth and position would be hereditary and privileged and the common man would have no say in who ruled the nation or how it was ruled. Under republicanism, the aristocracy would have no more rights than a common street laborer.

10. Answers may vary. The people of Paris are angry at their treatment by the aristocrats over the previous centuries, and they wish for revenge. Because many of them had been harshly ill-treated by the aristocrats, they wanted the aristocrats to suffer and die. Marguerite, in general wanted equality with the aristocrats and wanted their special privileges revoked so that all would be treated the same under the law, but she wanted the Marquis in particular to suffer for his treatment of Armand. Her actions are similar in motivation to the Parisians, though she did not want death, and she was against indiscriminate punishment. Her motivations are very similar, though much less vehement.

11. Answers may vary, but it appears that Sir Percy has deeper feelings for his wife than she or anyone else realizes, and those feelings probably will be revealed later in the story.

12. For all of these chapters, the author uses foreshadowing to encourage the reader to keep reading. At the end of Chapter 6 the author hints that Sir Percy still loves his wife passionately. In Chapter 8 the author hints that something about Chauvelin's conversation with Marguerite satisfied him or amused him, which makes us wonder what he has up his sleeve. At the end of Chapter 9, we know that Chauvelin has found information that he can use to force Marguerite to do as he wishes, and we wait to see how he will do this and how she will react.

Dig Deeper:

13. Answers will vary. Often the answer will depend on the situation. Can the result be foreseen, or is the result a logical conclusion of the action? Then one has little excuse. What was the attitude or intent of the person's actions? If we act in anger or spite, intending harm, then we have greater guilt. Was the result directly related to one's actions, or were one's actions a smaller part of a series of circumstances that led to a bad result? If our action directly results in a bad conclusion, we may be held more accountable, but if we were just a part of a series of circumstances, then our guilt be less. One might say that Marguerite should have known that her actions could or would have disastrous consequences because of the other executions in Paris and because of the strong political beliefs of some of her friends. She also was acting out of spite and hatred, and her actions directly led to the executions. On the other hand, she was young and inexperienced, she trusted her friends to act rationally, and the decision to execute the St. Cyrs was made by someone else. She definitely did not intend for the family of St. Cyr to be harmed or executed.

14. These verses warn us against holding grudges and taking revenge for ourselves; God declares that revenge is his right and responsibility. Instead we are supposed to love our neighbors, even those who do evil against us. We are supposed to love God, love our neighbor, do good, and live at peace as far as we are able. Answers may vary concerning how things would be different for Marguerite. However, if she had not held a grudge against the Marquis and try to take revenge for Armand, he and his family would not have died, she would not have been hated by the Comtesse, and perhaps her marriage to Sir Percy would have been far different, more loving, and more fulfilling.

15. Above all else, Marguerite wants love and adoration from Sir Percy. In fact, she wants near adoration and worship, which may not be healthy; but the healthy version of her desire is for his total love and dedication. Because she does not

get it from him, Marguerite insults and derides Sir Percy, trying to get him to react strongly to her.

16. According to Eph. 5:21–33, wives are supposed to submit and respect their husbands, and husbands are supposed to love their wives with the same selfless, all-encompassing love that Jesus Christ has for his church—in other words, husbands should have the same kind of love for their wives that caused Christ to die on the cross for us. This is exactly the kind of love that Marguerite desires from Sir Percy—total, complete, and passionate. However, she does not and has never given Sir Percy the respect that these verses command. She has always thought him foolish and only married him because she thought he would be totally devoted to her. Since his love has seemed to disappear, she has even begun to publicly disrespect him.

Chapters 10–13

Vocabulary:

1. lower-class, peasant; 2. indifferently, unemotionally, half-hearted; 3. wise, sensible, shrewd; 4. pretended, faked, simulated; 5. calmly, tranquilly, serenely; 6. showy, flamboyantly, gaudily; 7. motionless, still, immobile; 8. sophisticated, debonair, cultivated; 9. shrewd, sharp, clever; 10. clever, insightful, quick-witted; 11. ordinary, commonplace, routine; 12. disorder, turmoil, furor

Questions:

1. Chauvelin asks Marguerite to find out the identity of the Scarlet Pimpernel. Chauvelin has a letter written by Armand, her brother, making clear that he is at least helping, and may be a member of, the Scarlet Pimpernel's followers. By helping aristocrats escape France, Armand would be branded a traitor and executed. Chauvelin tells Marguerite that he will expose Armand if she does not help him.

2. Pretending to faint, Marguerite seeks Andrew's assistance. Andrew reads the note while Marguerite "recovers" herself, then he attempts to burn it. Marguerite snatches the paper from him and thanks him for finding a remedy—smoke from burning paper—for her giddiness. She deliberately upsets a table and a candelabra. Then while Andrew attends to the flame, Marguerite reads what remains of the note.

3. Marguerite learns that the Scarlet Pimpernel has told Sir Andrew that he will be in the supper-room at 1:00 a.m. in case Sir Andrew needs to meet with him.

Analysis:

4. The person described is Chauvelin. Answers may vary about why the author does not introduce him by name. By describing him again, rather than introducing him by name, Orczy further ingrains the negative impression of him with descriptions such as thin, small, shrewd, sarcastic, black, dark. Many of these words by themselves are innocent, but taken together make him seem sinister.

5. Answers will vary. Lady Portarles' statement is actually very pragmatic—she seems to be saying that the Comtesse will not accomplish what she wishes by her actions, so why make herself look foolish by acting in that way? She is not saying that they should pretend to be Lady Blakeney's friends nor that Lady Blakeney may behave badly without accountability because she is rich and popular. She is saying that the Comtesse's public snubs will not accomplish anything but make the Comtesse look foolish; therefore, she should stop her public accusations. However, there are times when we should and must stand up for what we believe to be right, whether we look foolish to some people or not. We must choose carefully the things we are willing to fight for and the way in which we choose to accomplish our goals.

6. S, M, M, S

7. Orczy says Marguerite had "the same feeling of good-humoured contempt which one feels for an animal or faithful servant." Answers will vary about what this reveals. Even if we ignore the word contempt, it appears that Marguerite views Sir Percy, her husband, in terms of what he gives or can do for her.

8. Frou-frou is the rustling sound of women walking in dresses. Frou-frou is an onomatopoeia because the word itself sounds like the sound it describes.

Dig Deeper:

9. At the end of these chapters, it appears Marguerite has chosen to save her brother Armand and will try to discover the identity of the Scarlet Pimpernel for Chauvelin. Answers about whether she chose wisely and students' choices will vary. By the nature of a moral dilemma, there can be more than one correct answer.

10. Answers will vary based on personal experience. Please treat students' answers as private and confidential.

11. When we are trying to determine our best course of action or to make tough decisions, these verses encourage us to use scripture to seek wisdom (Joshua 1:8, 2 Timothy 3:16), to seek advice and instruction from others (Proverbs 19:20),

and to pray for wisdom and guidance (James 1:5). Criteria for choosing between or amongst bad options in a moral dilemma will vary. After looking in the Bible, seeking advice, and praying, a hierarchical procedure for decision may follow these lines: 1) discard anything clearly forbidden in the Bible; 2) consider anything clearly recommended in the Bible; 3) prioritize based on what would be most honoring to God; 4) consider the advice and counsel of those who love you; 5) use the knowledge and wisdom God has given you to choose a course of action.

12. Answers may vary. Previous encounters with the Comtesse have revealed her belief that she is superior to some people and she is willing to publicly belittle them or insult them. They do not actually discuss whether she is virtuous. Based on our knowledge of the Comtesse, it is more likely that the Prince and Marguerite are actually discussing self-righteousness, which includes a sense of moral superiority to other people. Personal answers will vary. In general, self-righteousness is a negative characteristic because it looks down on other people, making other people feel bad. True virtue does not compare itself to others, it is just the commitment to do good and be good in one's self. Often true virtue will encourage virtue in others by being kind and an example, but a virtuous person concentrates on her own behavior, not the behavior of others.

Chapters 14–18
Vocabulary:
1. food; 2. ceaseless; 3. extract; 4. attempt; 5. boldness; 6. ambiguous; 7. copy; 8. agreeably; 9. lethargic; 10. muted; 11. contemptuous; 12. unfailing; 13. turbulent; 14. stubborn; 15. deceived; 16. whim; 17. opposing

Questions:
1. Chauvelin expects to see the notorious Scarlet Pimpernel, but he finds Sir Percy sleeping in the supper-room.
2. Sir Percy tells her he will take care of Armand. Later he slips a note for Marguerite under her door explaining that he must leave on business and will be gone for several days. He leaves by horse, then she hears later from his groom that he has boarded his yacht.
3. Marguerite is confused because Percy's study is austere and orderly, completely unlike the foppish simpleton ways he shows to her and the public. The study is clearly furnished for orderly business, with simple furniture and papers neatly arranged and organized.
4. Marguerite finds a signet ring with a scarlet pimpernel, implying that Sir Percy is the Scarlet Pimpernel.

Analysis:
5. a. S; b. S; c. S; d. M, M; e. M, M; f. M, M; g. M; h. M, M, S; i. S
6. Summaries will vary. Marguerite believes that her "woman's intuition" would immediately identify the Scarlet Pimpernel because she would recognize the greatness, the heroic nature of the man. This is ironic because it appears at the end of Chapter 18 as if Sir Percy is the Scarlet Pimpernel, and if so, then she has been living with him as his wife and never recognized him as a great man; in fact, she has believed he is a great fool.
7. In the last passage of Chapter 17, Orczy writes that Sir Percy, "so madly, blindly, passionately in love," knelt on the ground and kissed each spot where her feet had touched, and kissed the places where her hand had touched. This is an exaggerated action meant to emphasize the great feeling Sir Percy has for Marguerite. Orczy probably uses such exaggerated actions because to this point in the story the reader has not seen any real evidence of this love, and she wants to make certain the reader understands the depth of his feeling.
8. Answers may vary. The romantic element of this paragraph is closely associated with the hyperbole mentioned in the previous question. Sir Percy's actions—crawling on the ground kissing where Marguerite's feet had touched—are highly emotional, exaggerated, over the top, beyond what a real person would do. But the hyperbole and romanticism are effective because the reader fully understands now that Sir Percy deeply loves Marguerite.
9. Answers will vary. In the story, Bluebeard is a powerful French lord who has numerous wives who die young. He marries another young wife, and before going abroad for a time, leaves his wife the keys to the palace, warning her to never enter a certain room. The young wife's curiosity gets the better of her and she unlocks the room, finding in it the bodies of Bluebeard's previous wives hanging on the walls. She quickly leaves the room, but the key to the room falls on the floor and becomes stained with blood. When Bluebeard returns he sees the blood on the key and is about to kill his wife when her brothers break in and kill Bluebeard. She inherits all and eventually marries a good man. The allusion seems strange because there is nothing dangerous about Percy's room or Percy himself. Orczy may be simply playing up the suspense by alluding to a scary story with a common element, or she may be loosely linking to Chauvelin as Bluebeard and Percy as the rescuing brothers or as the good husband.
10. Answers will vary. Based on the signet ring, it appears that Sir Percy is the Scarlet Pimpernel. There are many clues

that seem more clear in retrospect than perhaps they did at the time: Percy's closest friends are all part of the league of the Scarlet Pimpernel; he is an expert boxer; he claims he cannot speak French well, yet he spent his childhood in France; he seems dull and stupid, yet he manages his many holdings very well and he regularly wins at cards. Students may list other clues. In general, he is believed to be stupid, but he manages to do very intelligent things.

Dig Deeper:

11. Personal answers will vary. Perhaps the best way to guard against the error of assuming we know all the answers is to consult more experienced people and listen to their advice. Getting wise counsel, particularly from solid Christian elders who have been in similar situations before, can give us a broader perspective and improve our ability to act wisely.

12. Fate means the development or manipulation of events beyond or outside a person's control, generally a generic supernatural power. Answers will vary. It is difficult to give credence to the fate statements when we can look back through the course of events and see how each development resulted from a specific choice and action. The execution of the Marquis de St. Cyr is a perfect example. Marguerite did not know that her statements would lead to his death, but in the current political climate a charge of treason against him could be reasonably assumed to lead to his death. Answers will vary concerning the question of whether Marguerite is responsible for her actions if fate "stepped in." If fate *controls* events and there is no option of deviating from fate's decrees, then it would seem logical that one is not responsible for what one cannot control. However, if fate determines the conclusion but not how that conclusion is reached, then one might still be held responsible for one's decisions.

13. Answers will vary. This is a version of a question that has occupied theologians and philosophers for centuries: Does man have free will? It will not be definitively answered here by reference to a few verses. However, the verses listed indicate that God has predetermined history and predestined his people, *and* he warns us to choose wisely and holds us accountable for our decisions. Sometimes, as in James 4, these paradoxical statements are right next to each other, indicating that the writers of scripture understood both to be true. We may, in the end, be left with this paradox, that God is in control, but he also somehow gives us free will, and how these things work together are beyond our current understanding.

14. In Chapter 18, Orczy repeatedly refers to pride being the great problem in their relationship. Marguerite's pride would not allow her to explain the circumstances of the de St. Cyr executions, and Sir Percy's pride would not allow him to demonstrate love for her under the circumstances. There may be some confusion over whether he asked for an explanation and was refused ("I entreated you for an explanation") or simply did not discuss it ("I *asked* for no explanation—I *waited* for one"). Marguerite viewed it as a test, apparently believing that if he truly loved her, he would accept her and not believe anything bad of her. Percy compares that to losing his honor and being "a dumb and submissive slave." Marguerite seems to overcome her pride better than Sir Percy, but he is distrustful of this change in her; he continues to hold back. Answers may vary about how they could have responded better, but if they had both responded with honesty and submission to each other, they probably would have avoided the entire problem. "Testing" each other's love is rarely a good idea because it easily leads to misunderstandings. If Percy wondered, he should have honestly asked. Marguerite should have clearly explained. Rather than respond with coldness and ridicule, seek clarity and resolution. Each became hurt in the marriage, and so each struck back in their own way. They did not try to actually solve the problem, they tried to "win."

Chapters 19–21

Vocabulary:

1. seclusion; 2. trivial; 3. compunction; 4. consummately; 5. poignancy; 6. paltry; 7. remorse; 8. raiment; 9. delude; 10. vestige; 11. atone; 12. appalling; 13. indefatigable; 14. wizened; 15. dulcet; 16. boisterous; 17. quandary; 18. profound

Questions:

1. Marguerite's suspicions that Percy is the Scarlet Pimpernel are solidified when Suzanne tells her that the Scarlet Pimpernel was in London that morning and had left for Calais, the same places to which Sir Percy was going. She decides Sir Percy is in imminent danger when Chauvelin sends her the letter that could have proved Armand's guilt in plotting with the Scarlet Pimpernel. Marguerite knows Chauvelin would not have given up the evidence unless he was convinced he was about to arrest the Scarlet Pimpernel.

2. Marguerite goes to Sir Andrew for help in saving the Scarlet Pimpernel. She knows that he is perhaps Percy's closest and most devoted friend, and she needs someone who knows Percy's plans and the places he will go so they can find and warn him.

3. Jellyband suspects that Marguerite and Sir Andrew are running away together, particularly because of the late-night rendezvous and because Sir Andrew is disguised as Marguerite's lacquey. Sir Andrew helps ease Jellyband's mind by paying him well, telling him how pleased Sir Percy will be because of the care Jellyband is taking of Marguerite, and asking

for separate rooms.

4. A terrible storm comes up from the French side of the Channel, keeping all boats from setting sail. Although it delays Marguerite and Sir Andrew, it also means Chauvelin cannot cross over to France and follow Sir Percy.

5. As they eat and wait for their rooms, Sir Andrew tells Marguerite of past escapades of Sir Percy as the Scarlet Pimpernel. He tells her of the many close escapes Sir Percy has had, the wily plots, and the many disguises he has employed. Sir Andrew probably does this to occupy Marguerite's mind and entertain her, but it also helps her to learn more about the daring side of Sir Percy's life, to get to know her husband better, and also to demonstrate what a brave, ingenious man Sir Percy is. This may ease her anxiety about Sir Percy's danger.

Analysis:

6. In the sentence from Chapter 19 Orczy anthropomorphizes the concepts of fate and nature, and she again anthropo-morphizes nature in the Chapter 21 reference. In all three cases she gives fate and nature intentionality or purpose to their actions or to circumstances. Fate "deals a blow," when fate is actually just a set of circumstances; nature "rises in revolt" as if it can think and rebel, then later it plays "a horrible, cruel trick" as if it intends to fool or thwart Marguerite. Neither of these things are alive and cannot act or plan; they are just ideas. Note, anthropomorphism is often confused with *personification* because both deal with things or ideas with human attributes. However, personification is actually a person or character that embodies or represents an idea or concept. Father Time, for example, personifies the passage of time. Hitler might be said to personify evil, or Romeo or Juliet to personify love. To personify is to embody an idea into a character, anthropomorphism simply has an object behaving in a humanlike manner.

7. According to this passage and the discussion in Chapter 4, both Marguerite and Lord Antony attribute the actions of Sir Percy and his followers to the love of "sport" and excitement. Answers will vary as to whether this is their true motiva-tion. Certainly it may be a significant part of it, or at least the fun part, but they also show a clear empathy for the French aristocrats and a strong desire to help them. However, because they, especially Lord Antony, have several times attributed the motivation to the love of excitement and sport, either answer is acceptable.

Dig Deeper:

8. Answers will vary. However, people generally discredit good works if the person doing them operates from selfish or self-serving motivation, such as their own pleasure or profit. This is often because such people are generally less trustwor-thy—if the fun or profit ends, so does their willingness to do the good work. However, if someone is acting altruistically, they are acting for the benefit of the person needing the help, not for their own benefit. In these cases, they generally continue to help even if it becomes difficult, dangerous, or troublesome.

9. *altruism:* unselfish or selfless concern and action for the well-being or welfare of others. *self-interest:* acting for personal interest or advantage, especially disregarding others' interests; *egoism:* valuing everything in reference to one's personal interest, ethical theory in which self-interest is the foundation of morality. a. E; b. A or E; c. E; d. E; e. A; f. E

10. Answers may vary somewhat. However, it has been pretty clear that in previous chapters Marguerite has judged her relationship with Sir Percy primarily by what she has or has not received from it; she punishes Sir Percy because he has not shown enough love toward her. She also has decided that she would betray the Scarlet Pimpernel and thereby save her brother, Armand, which also may be viewed as self-serving because she is willing to sacrifice others, including the Scarlet Pimpernel and French aristocrats, to save herself and her brother. However, in these chapters we see Marguerite's eyes opened to the true feelings and suffering of her husband and then to his true identity, at which point she becomes willing to sacrifice herself to save him. Suddenly she is aware of the personal tragedies her previous decisions may cause to people like Suzanne, and she is willing to fight and endure hardship and danger to prevent this.

11. Answers will vary. According to these verses, our primary motivation is to be like Christ, being willing to humble ourselves for the sake of others. Verse 3 tells us to do "nothing out of selfish ambition or vain conceit," but verse 4 tells us to act "not only [for] your own interests, but also [for] the interests of others." The scripture does not forbid our doing things for ourselves, but clearly says this should not be our focus. Our focus should be the benefit and well-being of oth-ers as we act in obedience to Christ. We are to use Jesus as our example, model, and guide for our behavior and attitudes.

Chapters 22–26

Vocabulary:

Sentences will vary but should show a good grasp of the meaning of the word. 1. subside, decrease, diminish; 2. speculation, guesswork; 3. cursory, brief, superficial; 4. squalid, filthy, shabby; 5. make-believe, acting, faking; 6. sullen, unfriendly, scowling; 7. impending, approaching; 8. indifference, lack of interest; 9. doubtfully, uncertainly, hesitantly; 10. curt, abrupt, blunt; 11. completely, absolutely, whole-heartedly; 12. spite, malevolence, evil intentions; 13. inadequate, scanty, insufficient; 14. charming, sophisticated, urbane; 15. courage, bravery, strength of character.

Questions:

1. When they arrive in Calais, Marguerite finds the country very changed. Instead of happy people, she finds everyone "wore a look of sly distrust" and a "look of fear and and of hate lurking in their brown eyes." The people spy on each to catch their enemies in indiscreet words or vulnerabilities, and they fear being caught in similar circumstances.

2. Brogard treats Marguerite and Sir Andrew with disdain and rudeness.

3. Brogard tells Marguerite and Sir Andrew that Sir Percy has been at the "Chat Gris" and will be back for dinner.

4. Chauvelin comes to the "Chat Gris" dressed as a priest.

5. Sir Percy puts pepper into his snuff and then offers some to Chauvelin. When Chauvelin sniffs it into his nose, the pepper hurts so badly that he is unable to pay attention to anything else, and Sir Percy simply walks out. *Note:* Some students may be familiar only with snuff as referring to dipping tobacco, which is put between the the cheek and gums. Snuff as referred to in the novel is a finely ground tobacco powder that is sniffed, or snorted, into the nose and sinus passages.

6. Desgas finds a Jewish man, Benjamin Rosenbaum, who says he saw Sir Percy rent a cart and horse from Reuben Goldstein and who knows how to get to Père Blanchard's hut. Chauvelin seems to detest the man, primarily because he is a Jew. To get the man to cooperate, Chauvelin gives him five gold pieces and promises 10 more if he will take them to the hut and if the trip is successful.

Analysis:

7. The cockade is a ribbon or knot of ribbons worn in a hat as a badge of office or to indicate allegiance or affiliation with a party. The tricolor cockade was the symbol of the French Revolution, combining the colors red and blue, symbolizing Paris, with royal white. The reference to wearing the cockade on the left side is more obscure, but probably is another reference of allegiance to the Revolution. The "right" generally referred to support for the established aristocracy and Christian religious structure, whereas "left" generally referred to opposition to the established orders or support for the Revolution. The wearing of the tricolor cockade was a statement that the wearer supported the Revolution, and wearing it on the left side of the hat further emphasized his support for the principles of the Revolution.

8. a. *Faggot* in this sentence refers to a bundle of sticks or firewood. Sometimes this word now is used as a slang insult for a homosexual male (interestingly, it began as an insult for a woman). Insults of any kind and against any person are wrong and demeaning. b. *Incontinently* in this sentence means without self-restraint or uncontrolled. Incontinence now often refers to not having control over one's urination or defecation.

9. Answers may vary slightly. Orczy continues this metaphor into the next chapter by naming Chapter 25 "The Eagle and the Fox." The third use of the metaphor refers to the "brave eagle" and "the ferret's trap." In each instance, Sir Percy is an eagle, but the metaphor for Chauvelin keeps changing. First he is a rat, then a fox, then a ferret. Answers for the reason for this will vary; accept reasonable answers. Orczy is illustrating different attributes of Chauvelin and emphasizing them in different situations. She uses the rat as a metaphor as Marguerite looks upon him and finds him disgusting. He becomes the fox (which may be an ironic reference because of the way Sir Percy toys with him) as Chauvelin tries to match wits with Sir Percy. He then becomes a ferret, which is a weasel, quiet, predatory, and ferocious.

10. Sir Percy enters the "Chat Gris" singing "God Save the King." In this chapter Percy acts in such a way toward Chauvelin as to keep him off balance. For example, singing "God Save the King" in France at this time would be almost a slap in the face, or at least very shocking, because they had just killed their king, imprisoned the royal family, and were hunting and killing the aristocrats. Percy also immediately recognizes Chauvelin even though Chauvelin is heavily disguised as a priest. He slaps Chauvelin on the back as Chauvelin is taking a mouthful of soup, speaks of a man dying from choking on soup, and sits down to eat with him. Percy several times mispronounces Chauvelin's name, asks him about being a priest, pretends that Chauvelin might be meeting a woman, which would be an issue if Chauvelin were a priest, and acts as if he has all day and nowhere to go. Percy acts as if he were very friendly toward Chauvelin but is a bit of a fool, saying and doing all the wrong things. However, almost everything he does is calculated to confuse and keep Chauvelin off balance, a little anxious, and not as alert as he might otherwise be.

Dig Deeper:

11. Illustrations will vary. Some examples include: "these men at this moment await with perfect confidence and unshaken faith the arrival of the Scarlet Pimpernel, who has pledged his honour to take them safely across the Channel"; "Sir Percy Blakeney would not be the trusted, honoured leader of a score of English gentlemen . . . if he abandoned those who placed their trust in him. As for breaking his word, the very thought is preposterous!"; "with . . . this worship of his

own word of honour, . . . Blakeney would brave any danger, run the wildest risks sooner than break it, . . . to rescue those who trusted in him." Sir Percy will keep his word no matter what the risk or cost to himself. He values honor and trustworthiness. He will let down neither his men nor others who trust him.

12. Both the Psalm and Matthew passages deal with telling the truth and keeping our word, and both either say outright or imply that we are to keep our word even when it is inconvenient or even actually painful. As Christians we are always to do exactly what we say we are going to do (let your "yes be yes, and your no be no"). This is one of the primary reasons Percy is such a great leader and so completely trusted. To him, the very idea of breaking his word or breaking the trust of someone is ridiculous. He keeps his word even at great risk and pain to himself, and for this men trust him and are willing to place even their lives in his hands.

13. Answers will vary. Brogard seems to believe that freedom means not doing what others want you to do or not showing civility to anyone. He seems to connect being civil or polite with being obsequious or servile, so to make sure people do not think he is servile, he is rude and uncooperative. He behaves rudely to show that he is their equal and does not have respect others' wishes or comfort ("the man stood and lounged about, smoking his evil-smelling pipe, sometimes under Marguerite's very nose, as any free-born citizen who was anybody's equal should do"). Examples may include: "it was not for a free citizen to show deference, or even courtesy, to anyone"; "It took Brogard some few moments to consider the question. A free citizen does not respond too readily to the wishes of those who happen to require something of him"; "Brogard leant up against the table, smoking and looking down superciliously at these two *sacrrrés Anglais*"; "The heaven-born messenger of bliss spat upon the floor, to express his contempt for all and sundry *aristos,* who chose to haunt the 'Chat Gris'"; "with a surly gesture, he shook off from his arm that pretty hand which princes had been proud to kiss"; "He did not think that it was fitting for a citizen—who was the equal of anybody—to be thus catechised by these *sacrrés aristos,* . . . It was distinctly more fitting to his newborn dignity to be as rude as possible; it was a sure sign of servility to meekly reply to civil questions"; "And with this parting assertion of his rights as a citizen and a free man, to be as rude as he well pleased, Brogard shuffled out of the room." As to why he behaves this way, answers may vary. The peasants of France had suffered great indignities under much of the aristocracy for generations, and it is possible that they were exhibiting the behavior that was modeled to them; they behaved this way about freedom because this is how the aristocrats had behaved to them. Brogard also may be exercising his "right to be rude" because he has had so few rights in the past and is now going to go to the extreme in his use of them. Also, France was in turmoil, with many in government and the community fanatically rooting out any semblance of the old aristocratic regime, and so some people may demonstrate their allegiance to the new regime by very visibly and emphatically rejecting anything to do with the old regime, such as Brogard does here, by being rude or antagonistic to anyone or anything that might be connected to it, such as any *aristos*. He also simply may be a very unpleasant, rude man, and this "freedom" makes him feel he can indulge this behavior because it is his "right."

14. Answers will vary. The 1 Peter passage discusses God's bringing freedom to and galvanizing Christians into his people, in a sense freeing us from the world, and then tells us to submit to worldly authorities so that they will see the goodness of God in us. We are to use our freedom but not abuse it. The remaining verses also describe how we are to use our freedom to emphasize the mercy, grace, and power of God by building up each other, working for the good of others. This also fits well within the parameters of "love your neighbor as yourself" and "do to others what you would have them do to you," some of the greatest commandments of the Bible. Brogard's attitude toward freedom is in direct opposition to these verses. He seems to value it only as it applies to himself and does not use his freedom to be kind or to build up others. His freedom seems to contain a fear that it must be guarded and hoarded.

Chapters 27–31
Vocabulary:
1. c; 2. a; 3. c; 4. b; 5. d; 6. a; 7. b; 8. c; 9. a; 10. d; 11. a; 12. b; 13. b; 14. c
Questions:
1. Marguerite starts following Chauvelin and the cart, keeping within the sound of the cart so she does not get too close nor too far away.
2. The Jewish man, Benjamin Rosenbaum, acts as guide to take Chauvelin to Père Blanchard's hut, but it is actually Sir Percy in disguise. When they arrive at the hut, Chauvelin has Rosenbaum tied up, and when he learns that Percy and his men have escaped, Chauvelin has his soldiers beat Rosenbaum severely.
3. The men waiting in the hut escape to Sir Percy's yacht. Sir Percy, disguised as Benjamin Rosenbaum, was able to slip out of his ropes and deliver a note to the men in the hut, instructing them to slip out and go down to the yacht. Because the sol-

diers were specifically told to do nothing until the tall Englishman arrived, they did nothing about the men leaving the hut.

4. When Marguerite hears someone singing "God Save the King," she runs to the hut screaming that they are betrayed and begging Armand to fight. She cries out to Percy to flee. Chauvelin's men grab her and silence her. As to whether she helps or hurts the Scarlet Pimpernel, answers may vary, but her crying out gives the perfect excuse for Chauvelin and his men to assume he has been warned off and has escaped. Her warning would seem to fit right into Percy's plan.

5. Sir Percy gave instructions to Sir Andrew to travel to the hut by a long, circuitous route so that he was unlikely to meet with any of Chauvelin's soldiers and so that Sir Andrew would arrive after the action was done so he could help Sir Percy escape at the end. Sir Andrew is able to help Percy and Marguerite get down to the yacht waiting for them. In the note, Sir Percy had written that his men were to meet him near the "Chat Gris," so Chauvelin dashes off to catch him there. The note is a decoy, however, and Percy's men sail out of sight, then come back for him. The author does not say exactly what happens to Chauvelin, only that he is never seen in London again.

Analysis:

6. The Amalekites were a nomadic people of the Negev, mentioned in the Bible (Numbers 13:29). The specific allusion here would be the treachery they practiced on the Israelites as they left Egypt and traveled to the Promised Land. In Deuteronomy 25:17–18, the Israelites are told to remember how the Amalekites harried and killed the stragglers in the Jewish camp as they traveled. In 1 Samuel 15:2, God promises to punish the Amalekites for killing helpless Israelites during the exodus and for the harassing raids and destruction they continued on Israel even up to the time of Saul. The Jewish man here would be calling Reuben an Amalekite because of the Amalekites' reputation for treachery and predation. It would be a significant insult.

7. a. S; b. A; c. S; d. A, M; e. M; f. S; g. M, S; h. S

8. Percy chose the guise of a Jewish man because, according to the author, he knew the French very well and he knew how they despise the Jews. Percy believed Chauvelin would hate the Jewish man so much that he would not pay much attention to him and would not want to get too close to him; therefore the risk of discovery was very low. He played to the prejudices of Chauvelin by being cringing and loathsome, as Chauvelin would expect a Jew to be. The disguise worked very well; Chauvelin saw him only as a stereotype and not as a person, and therefore never suspected that he could be the Scarlet Pimpernel.

9. Bigotry is intolerance toward those who hold different opinions from or are different from ourselves. It assumes that all other opinions are wrong and differences from us are bad. Prejudice is a preconceived opinion that is not based on reason or actual experience and dislike or hostility based on such an opinion. The biggest difference is that stereotype is simply attributing certain characteristics to a group of people, whereas bigotry and prejudice assumes negative attributes toward a group of people and positions oneself as superior. For example, "People who wear red shirts are stylish" is a stereotype, but not bigoted or prejudiced. "People who wear green shirts are crazy and should be kept off the street" is a stereotype, but it is also bigotry and prejudice because it is intolerant, hostile, and assumes superiority over people who wear green shirts. Chauvelin attributed a lot of characteristics to Rosenbaum, and to Jews in general, that had little basis in fact. He was hostile to Rosenbaum before Rosenbaum had even spoken. All of Chauvelin's actions toward Rosenbaum were based on negative stereotypes and were bigoted and prejudiced. Chauvelin hated Rosenbaum before he even met him because he had already attributed a lot of negative characteristics to him, based on negative assumptions about his race as a whole. Sir Percy was able to use this bigoted blindness to his advantage by acting out all the negative stereotypes Chauvelin already expected.

Dig Deeper:

10. Answers may vary, but may include: dirty, mock humility, obsequiousness, shuffling, patient, greedy, sneaky, malignant or vengeful, cowardly, lazy.

11. Answers may vary, accept reasonable answers. Percy knew that Chauvelin, because he assumes all Jews have a certain set of negative characteristics, would not notice any details about this particular Jew if he acted like Chauvelin's prejudiced stereotype. Chauvelin's bigotry dictated what a Jew would look like and how he would act, and if this man looked and acted like the stereotype, then Chauvelin would not think about or examine him too closely. Percy made sure the Jewish man he pretended to be looked and acted in a manner consistent with the bigotry and prejudice Chauvelin believed. Percy exploited Chauvelin's prejudices against the Jews. When Chauvelin looked at "the Jew," he saw only the negative stereotypes he believed about Jews, he did not see an individual man.

12. Answers will vary based on personal experience.

13. Answers may vary. At the time of Jesus, the Jews and the Samaritans were hostile to each other. Jews viewed

Samaritans as worse than Gentiles because they were half-breeds, Jews who had not remained pure either in their lineage or in their worship of God. Therefore, it is significant that Jesus chooses as his hero this man who would be looked down on, and even hated, by his Jewish audience. He turned the prejudice on its ear by having the Samaritan act in a godly manner when the religious Jews in the story do not. Jesus was using someone they despised to be a model for them, someone he was telling them to pattern their lives after. Jesus was telling them, and us, to put aside our prejudice and bigotry, to look past the outward appearance or our preconceived ideas, to see the real person. All men are our neighbors, and God commands us to love them as we love and care for ourselves. See also Matthew 22:34–40.

Overview

1. Answers will vary. *Marguerite:* She fell in love with, or liked the love she received from, Percy and decided to marry him. Around the time of the wedding she told Percy about her role in the death of the Marquis de St. Cyr and his family, but did not explain the full circumstances. He grew withdrawn from her, which confused and angered her, so she began to deliberately embarrass and provoke him. After Chauvelin coerces her cooperation, Marguerite turns to Percy for help and comfort, and in his response recognizes the repressed love she thought had died. She begins to thaw toward him and to wish him well, and she determines to reawaken his love for her. When she learns Percy is the Scarlet Pimpernel, her love awakens in a fierce and passionate flame and she decides she must save him or die with him. From this point on, Marguerite holds Percy in the highest respect and admiration and is willing to die with or for him. *Percy:* Percy has maintained a charade of foolishness to mask his role as the Scarlet Pimpernel, but he also revealed some wit and intelligence to Marguerite. He loved her for her intelligence and insight, and proposed marriage. However, around the time of the wedding, he learned of her role in the St. Cyr family executions, and when he did not receive a full explanation from her, he feared she might discover and reveal his secrets, so he pushed her away by becoming uncaring, banal, and completely proper. In his pride he would not confront her about her role, instead choosing to close off and conceal his love and appear loveless and witless so she would not get close enough to learn his secrets. His resolve and his mask begin to crack when Marguerite opens her heart to him in the garden, but he immediately leaves to save Armand and the others in France. When she arrives in France and he sees the she is acting on and risking herself for her love, he finally relents and reveals his love for her and renounces his pride. Answers will vary concerning students' responses to the characters' actions.
2. Answers will vary; accept well-reasoned and documented answers. The Baroness seems to hold somewhat to the "women are the weaker sex" position, though she clearly has a smart, brave woman as one of her main characters. Marguerite is preyed upon by Chauvelin, who uses her sisterly, or maternal, love for Armand as a lever against her. She seems to be ruled more by passion than the male characters and to be more spiteful. There are also several instances in which Orczy refers to the rescues in France and the trip to Calais as "man's work" and states late in the novel that "Marguerite was as calm, as clear-headed as any man." Though she does go to France to save Sir Percy, in the end it might appear her work was ultimately unnecessary and it is again Sir Percy who saves the day. A strong argument could be made that Marguerite is a strong heroine at a time when strong heroines were not as fashionable, and she takes control of the situation and becomes leader over Sir Andrew, but there yet remains a recurring tendency for the heroine to be rescued or enlightened by the hero, implying a prejudice toward the strong male leader role. However, because of the strength of Marguerite and some of the instances noted above, a good case can be made for Orczy focussing on a strong female character. Accept well reasoned and well-supported answers.
3. The protagonists are Sir Percy and Marguerite, though others such as Sir Andrew and Lord Antony may be listed as secondary protagonists. Marguerite may be considered by some to be an antagonist for the first half, but this would be a slight misunderstanding of the character. The clear antagonist of the novel is Chauvelin, who hunts the Scarlet Pimpernel and manipulates Marguerite. Answers may vary about the main protagonist. Sir Percy, the Scarlet Pimpernel, is an obvious choice. The novel is titled after him and his adventures provide the nucleus around which the plot revolves. However, some students may note that the character who takes up the bulk of the novel is Marguerite, and most of the action is shown from her general point of view. In truth, the story is less about the exploits of the Scarlet Pimpernel and more about the resolution of the relationship between Sir Percy and Marguerite. Accept reasonable answers.
4. Answers may vary. The student should recognize this as an epiphany, though it may seem like a "slow" epiphany. Dramatic tension does rise somewhat before Marguerite's realization, but it does not raise the expectation that the complication or danger has been resolved as would a false climax; in fact, the realization that Sir Percy is the Scarlet Pimpernel *raises* the levels of complication and danger. The realization *does* change our perception of the relationships in the story and the dangers to come, as expected from an epiphany.

5. Answers will vary in all particulars. Chauvelin does seem to view people as tools or objects, with little concern for them. Orczy mentions several times in the story that his whole being is wrapped up in catching "enemies" of France, no matter how he can accomplish it. He is willing to sacrifice his spies and to use the threat of killing Armand to force Marguerite to spy against her friends and husband, yet he is also willing to let release Armand, who he views as a traitor to France, to capture the Scarlet Pimpernel. He forces Marguerite to go against all she believes in and manipulates her into betraying her husband. He then manipulates her love for both her husband and brother to keep her silent. He regularly threatens everyone he deals with, particularly those under him or those over whom he has the advantage, such as Desgas, the soldiers, and Benjamin Rosenbaum. Chauvelin threatens his underlings and soldiers with death even for things outside of their control. He had Benjamin Rosenbaum beaten severely, even though he had fulfilled his part of the bargain. Chauvelin's attitude and actions toward people instills fear, but not respect or love or even camaraderie. He is obeyed, but he is not liked. Even Brogan the pub keeper and his wife feared and avoided Chauvelin.

6. Answers may vary about the foil/parallelism because the scenes and situations have elements of both. It has the elements of a foil in that the scenes contrast so greatly, bringing out the comfort and conviviality of the British inn and the poverty and hostility of the French inn. They also have elements of parallelism in the way they represent their respective nations and populations. Answers may vary. The correlation between England and the characters and "The Fisherman's Rest" is clear because Orczy describes Jellyband as "John Bull," a stereotype of the common Englishman. The inn is orderly, busy, and comfortable. The furnishings and utensils are well used but also well cared for, described as gleaming and rich. The food is hearty and the beer notable. "The Fisherman's Rest" is also busy, with men of several stations present, from local laborers and tradesmen to nobility. Jellyband is cheerful, hospitable, and expansive in his coffee-room, talking with everyone and being solicitous without being subservient. He is polite and hearty with all, but respectful of those of higher rank, including Sir Percy, Marguerite, Sir Andrew, and the others. The "Chat Gris" is less obviously made to represent France, but in the paragraphs leading to the introduction of the inn, the description of the people and streets of Calais are similar to the descriptions of the inn. The "Chat Gris" is dismal, dingy, and dirty; the furnishings are broken, torn, and stained. Only the food is described as passable. Brogard, the landlord, is similarly filthy and stained, but he makes up for it by being rude, unpleasant, and surly. The inn is empty; the only patrons are the English "*aristos*" and Chauvelin and his men. The two inns are almost complete opposites, even down to their names: "The Fisherman's Rest" has a peaceful, "rest at the end of the day" sound; "Chat Gris" means gray cat, implying, perhaps, a certain drab aloofness. As for the inns representing the nations of England and France, the descriptions align with other statements about the countries and their inhabitants in other parts of the novel. This is most obvious in the first chapter of the novel concerning the scenes in Paris, and the paragraphs leading up to Marguerite's arrival in the "Chat Gris." Clearly Orczy believed, as generalizations, that the people of England at the time were well fed, hearty, free souls who were at peace with themselves and each other, even if somewhat quaint or insular, but the people of France were suspicious, frightened, and, perhaps, viciously defensive, leading to a certain breakdown and degradation of society.

7. Answers may vary. Brogard seems to regard freedom as the right to be dismissive and rude to others, proving that they have no authority over him and are not better than he is. He treats Marguerite and Sir Andrew with disdain and rudeness, purposely giving them bad service to prove he can do what he wants. However, when Chauvelin arrives, Brogard clearly becomes frightened. He serves Chauvelin quickly and then disappears as quickly as he can to keep himself out of harm's way. Brogard's freedom obviously does not mean much when Chauvelin is around, which implies that his freedom is false, that he has traded one master for another. Orczy may be implying the same for the entire nation, that France had traded the aristocracy for ideological taskmasters, a new elite just as oppressive as the former.

8. Answers will vary based on the theme chosen by the student. Accept reasonable, well-supported answers.

9. Answers will vary.

10. Answers will vary, but some contrivances might be Chauvelin's arrival at the "Chat Gris"; Percy's ability to escape from Chauvelin at the "Chat Gris" and also escape from the approaching soldiers; Percy's ability to disguise himself as Benjamin Rosenbaum and return with the soldiers in so short an amount of time; Chauvelin not recognizing Percy as Rosenbaum even though they are specifically hunting Percy; Marguerite not recognizing Percy; Chauvelin taking Percy/Rosenbaum with him, even to the hut; Percy/Rosenbaum's ability to get loose from the ropes; Percy's ability to approach the hut without being detected and slip the note into the hut; Marguerite not noticing Percy/Rosenbaum leaving or coming back; Percy's ability to escape his bonds to approach the hut, but inability to get loose after he is beaten; the French soldiers allowing all of the men in the hut to leave without raising any sort of alarm or protest. Answers will vary as to whether Orczy was successful.